Other Books by E. Prybylski

Boston Blight

Smoke & Magic
- Fallen
- Hot & Cold

Frost & Shadow
- Cold Front

How to Finish the Damn Book
- How to Write the Damn Book
- How to Publish the Damn Book

Short Story Collections
- When Nightmares Fall — Edited by Elizabeth Harvey
- Damn Faeries — Edited by Elizabeth Harvey
- Invisible, Not Imagined — Edited by Rock and Roll Saved My Soul
- Fields of Broken Steel — Edited by M. Ngai
- Daughter of Spring — Edited by N.D. Gray
- Scion of Summer — Edited by N.D. Gray
- Heir of Autumn — Edited by N.D. Gray
- Ink Stained and Spellbound — Edited by N.D. Gray
- Sister Death — Edited by N.D. Gray
- Halls of Ghostly Holly — Edited by N.D. Gray

HOW TO WRITE THE DAMN BOOK

A guide to getting the damn story out of your brain

Ellis Prybylski

HOW TO WRITE THE DAMN BOOK. Copyright © 2024 Ellis Prybylski. All Rights Reserved. No part of this book may be used or reproduced in any manner except brief quotations without written permission. For information, contact E. Prybylski.

Edited by: Mel Ngai
Cover by: E. Prybylski

Fonts Used:
Angleterre Book
Century Gothic
Georgia

www.ehprybylski.com

ISBN Print: 9798987571958
ISBN Ebook: 9798987571941

Contents

Introduction ——————— 7

Chapter One ——————— 9
Idea Generation and Planning

Where Ideas Come From..9
Planning Base Elements (Fiction).. 15
Planning Base Elements (Non-Fiction) 20
Plotter vs. Discovery Writer 23
The Principle of Outlines..24

Chapter Two ——————— 29
Story Craft and the Star Point Method

The Function of Tension 29
The Points of the Star 34
Using the Points 38

Chapter Three ——————— 41
Researching For Your Book

What You Need to Research...42
Choosing Your Sources..46
How to Organize Your Research 51
When to Stop Researching 52

Chapter Four   56
The Drafting Process

Writing Programs 56
Sustainable Writing Habits 60
Why Comparison Kills Creativity.. 67
Flow States and Focus Techniques 69
How Many Words Should "X" Be?... 75
Combating Writer's Block 78
The Act Two Slump 82

Chapter Five —— 86
Self-Editing

The Importance of Emotional Distance...................................86
Tools and Programs.. 88
Types of Editing...92
Self-Developmental Editing 95
Self-Line Editing..97
Self-Copy Editing... 104
How to Stop Editing 105

Chapter Six —— 108
Beta Reading

Why Beta Readers Matter 108
Working With Beta Readers..109
Where to Find Beta Readers 113
What to Do With the Feedback 115

Chapter Seven —— 119
Final Touches

Considering a Series 120
Paths to Publishing... 122
When to Start Marketing.. 128
Final Considerations 130

Appendix —— 132
Books on Craft 132
Writing Software 132
Editing Software 133
Marketing 133

Introduction

The journey of writing a book is a long one. If you are starting it, you are one of the few and mighty. Many people think they might like to write a book, but very few ever go from that first inkling of interest to finishing their project. Whether you have completed your first draft, your third draft, or you're buying this guide because you have just decided to get serious about writing, you are in the minority chasing their dreams of publication.

Before we get too far in, I should introduce myself. I'm E. I've been a professional editor since the early 2000s and have worked both freelance and with indie presses during that time. I am also an author in my own right and have an urban fantasy series along with a number of short stories in various anthologies around the literary world.

In 2023, I and several others founded the Neurodivergent Publishing Conference—a conference for neurodivergent folks in the publishing sphere to network, learn, and grow together in a place by and for us.

Outside of the writing and editing sphere, I am a tabletop role-playing game (TTRPG) nerd, a historical reenactor (SCAdian), a herder of cats, a violinist, and a partner to an excellent husband. I am autistic, have ADHD, and am physically disabled and very open about all those things. Not because I particularly want attention but because I try to be a voice about those topics in the world. I am also LGBTQ+, and if any of those things make you recoil in horror, there's a good chance I'm not going to be a good fit for you on your journey. I do wish you luck, though.

This is a roadmap intended to help you find direction in the process of writing your book. There are so many works about the craft itself, specific elements thereof, and other particulars that I am unsure, at this juncture, I have anything to add that hasn't already been said.

However, I have *not* seen a direct guide on how to avoid common pitfalls, what the flow of writing and planning should be, and how to get through writing a book from start to finish. The second volume of this series will focus on what to do once you've written it, so don't worry. I'm not leaving you high and dry with a manuscript and no direction when you've finished.

It is my hope that this work will be of use to you. For all my tongue-in-cheek jokes, puns, or humor, I genuinely do love teaching authors. Many writers encounter similar trials and struggles along the path to publishing, and my goal is to help you sidestep some of those.

Chapter One
Idea Generation and Planning

Before we write the book, we need to have an idea. This idea might be as simple as, "I want to write a book about writing" or as complex as, "I want to write an urban fantasy series about fallen angels in a world where magic is all over the place, and..." These ideas don't appear to us in a vacuum, however.

These first steps taken toward writing your story will give you the foundation to write everything else and a platform from which to launch your book. In this chapter, I'm going to go over where ideas come from, what the basic elements and questions are for writing a book, and then some story craft ideas.

For the non-fiction writers in the audience here, please note that there *is* a segment dedicated to non-fiction in this chapter after the bits about fiction. I promise I have not forgotten you!

Where Ideas Come From

The first step in writing any book—fiction or non-fiction—is to come up with ideas for what you want to say. In non-fiction, it might be a particular subject you have expertise in or a story you want to share, and for fiction, it's based on a tale you have to tell. One way or another, you'll need to come up with that idea. I see writing groups flooded with people who aren't sure how that process works, so let's open this journey with thinking about places our ideas come from and busting some myths about story concepts in general.

Your book idea doesn't have to be "unique."

This is one of the biggest mistakes I see people making when trying to come up with plans for a story. Uniqueness is valuable, and I wouldn't tell people to eschew what makes them unique. However, people often come up with some outrageous ideas in their quest to be unique. They bend their stories into pretzels and try and mash a bunch of genres together to create Something Never Before Seen on Live TV.

The thing is, very few ideas are entirely "new." Most stories have been told before, at least in the broad strokes of them, and very few concepts are truly revolutionary. *That is okay.* One of the biggest sources of inspiration for creatives is other creatives, which means we all have influences and ideas from things we've encountered in the world. They all bleed into us, and we create something new out of them. That's the nature of the game.

This guide you're reading right now isn't giving information never before seen by anybody in the writing world. The thing that makes this book different from others is how *I* put it together. That, and it being a distillation of my personal experience as an author, so I may have perspectives others do not. Fiction is the same. If you're telling a story that has been told before (people falling in love, fantasy stories about dragons, a story about people fighting wars in space, etc.), the key will be how *you* tell it. It's *your voice* that makes the story unique. And that is more than enough.

Beg, borrow, and steal concepts from media you love.

To be abundantly clear, I am not advocating plagiarism. However, art is a never-ending loop of being inspired by other things. How many times have you been exposed to something and said, "But what if…?" and then had a story idea?

As I stated in the previous section, every artist, author, musician, and pretty much anyone who does creative work draws from things they have seen before. We gather all

Idea Generation and Planning

these ideas, moments, thoughts, and experiences together and build them into something entirely our own. Think of it like Legos. The pieces are all the different media and ideas you have come into contact with over the course of your life. While many people may be using the same bricks (same color or shape), how you combine them is what creates something new. That's where your own creativity comes in.

You also have a blend life experiences unique to you that you can draw from and will inherently lean into. That blend of experiences, understanding, and ideas will shape your voice and what stories you tell, not to mention how you tell them. Putting a huge amount of effort into chasing uniqueness is a bit of a mistaken prospect. The best way to cultivate that is through leaning into your own strengths, experiences, and story. Your author voice already *is* unique because you are the only you in existence.

Consume media in the genre(s) you want to write in.

While of course reading (which I include audiobooks into) is one of the things on top of my list of things writers should be doing, I consider consuming *any* media to be valuable. Particularly if it's in the genre you intend to write in. That can include video games, reading, television series, movies, podcasts, articles, and anything else related to what you want to write.

Contrary to what many people think, I believe there's a lot to be learned from mediums other than books when it comes to storytelling. Recently, video games have been really kicking up their game. *Red Dead Redemption 2* has one of the best stories I've ever experienced, and the characters are richly layered, well created, have arcs, and the narrative is excellent. I've had similar experiences with *Dragon Age, Mass Effect, Stray, Control,* and many other games. Movies and television shows may use words differently than text does, but you can learn a lot about dialogue, characterization, story structure, and foreshadowing through them. I actually consider *Avatar: the Last Airbender* to be a storytelling master class.

Now, there *are* some things you can only learn from reading books in your genre. However, if you want to spark ideas and creativity, you don't need to limit yourself to just reading in order to find inspiration.

What you *do* get from books and nowhere else are things like specific elements of the craft and genre expectations for things created in book form. You also learn how pacing works in novel form and what the story beats are and where they should be. You can learn a lot about story structure from other mediums, but novel pacing is a unique creature. Knowing where you should be at whatever-thousand-words is something you can only learn from reading.

Consider how you consume your media.

Now that we've established that I mean *all media*, let's take a look at something a little more specific. When I talk about how you consume your media, I don't mean what format it is in. I mean how you interact with it. As authors do what amounts to research and idea gathering, we want to approach the media we consume with a bit more of a clinical eye than we might if we were interacting with it for pure pleasure.

Think of it as the difference between a chef doing a taste test at a restaurant and trying to identify how a dish was made instead of a layperson eating the meal because it tastes good. When we consume media through the lens of wanting to write, we must be as the chef doing a taste test. Of course we should enjoy it, but we must *also* think about how the narrative is constructed, what techniques the creators have used, and how elements are brought together to create the whole.

Doing this with media you're familiar with is a great place to start because honestly, you know it well enough to recognize the beats and know the story. Breaking it down into what you enjoy about it and studying how they accomplished what you enjoy is useful data collection.

One thing to know about this process, however, is that *it will forever change how you interact with media.* At this point in my life, it's very rare that a story in any medium can pull a plot twist on me that I don't see a million miles away. I know how the sauce is created, so trying to surprise me with it is not an easy feat. It's certainly *possible*, but it's not easy. You will end up in a similar space as you continue your journey and study the craft.

When you reach that head space, know that your enjoyment of media doesn't vanish. I still enjoy movies and games and the twists they tell. I still love their narratives. Knowing things doesn't make me enjoy them less.

I'm about to drop some *Red Dead Redemption 2* spoilers in the next paragraph. The game was released in 2018, so I don't feel like I'm doing anyone a disservice, but if you haven't played it and want to, well... skip the example.

— SPOILER —

In *Red Dead Redemption 2*, there is a scene early on in the game where the main character, Arthur Morgan, encounters a very sick person. He's doing a job and ends up with that sick person coughing on him. This happens in the first quarter of the game; it's one of the initial quests. It's not one you can miss because it's a story quest. You have to do it.

The minute that quest happened in that way, I knew that Arthur was going to die of tuberculosis. There was no avoiding it. And I knew instantly how the story was going to use that moment as a pivotal one in the narrative. Now, the game has a few specific flavor endings. You can either spend most of the game making altruistic choices and have Arthur kind of try to redeem himself right to the end, or you can say "to hell with it" and have him go out the selfish bastard he starts as. But the result is still the same. Arthur has to choose how he's going to use the time he has left. That's the part that's up to the player.

—SPOILER END—

Now, that knowledge didn't make me enjoy the game any less. In fact, I cried several times throughout it and spent extra time in that game doing every single side quest, catching every single big fish, and hunting every single big-game animal. I am not usually a completionist gamer, but the game and story were just that good.

When we're analyzing these things for ideas and for our study, we have to ask ourselves *why* they're that good. What about that media draws us and creates a spark that rages into a fire of fandom? I can answer that question about all the media I really love. So while you're looking for ideas and dabbling in the waters of starting your book, that's some work you're going to want to do.

Don't ask for feedback on early concepts from the public.

Seriously. Don't. People pour into writing groups all the time, throwing their ideas into the ether, and a large percentage of the time, they're shot down before they write a word. The world is not kind to half-baked ideas, which is where we *all* start. There's a very good chance you'll walk away from that experience feeling like someone ran you over with an 18-wheeler.

It's not that I think soliciting advice is a bad plan, but recognize that early on, you may not yet have the faith in yourself to write your story. At that point, it's easy to be swayed by people who have alternate opinions. And let's be honest: *everyone has opinions.* Many of which are less than helpful. It is, in fact, quite rare that people's opinions on the very early stages of a book are of any use whatsoever, so it's better not to ask.

The exception to this is if you have a small writing group of people you know where you can toss ideas around. I run a group like that on Discord where people form friendships and then mull over ideas in chat and talk through things. Nobody is there to tap dance on anybody else's dreams. No one is there to just stomp on folks. And nobody is really allowed to critique initial ideas. Sometimes, we find holes in it and talk things over, but there's no bashing.

You can also solicit help from a book coach or developmental editor. We can help you refine your idea into a place to start. Even then, our advice is only so helpful because this is *your* vision. When I'm helping someone write their draft, my job is mostly to ask questions for them to answer and help them learn how to answer those questions in their work. I don't dictate what they do with their story, but I open doors and give them some direction on how to form their project.

The time for asking for feedback *will* come, but it's not this stage of writing. When you're working on your first novel, it's tempting to see if people like your idea. Unfortunately, it's rare that you can lay out the entire idea to everyone in a way that matches what's in your head. As a result, people's evaluation is based on half-baked thoughts and their feedback will discourage you more often than not.

Planning Base Elements (Fiction)

Once you've gathered your ideas and have a rough concept, the next step is planning. This is where I may lose some of you who just want to get into writing the dang book, particularly you ADHD folks. I see you. I *am* you. Keep in mind that in this section, I'm not talking about outlining. I have a whole section on that coming up, so don't run away screaming just yet. I'll let you know when. I promise.

When I talk about planning your book, this *can* certainly include an outline, but before you start doing that, you should do more foundation work. There are some core questions you need to answer before you get to the more specific task of designing your plot.

For non-fiction writers, your segment is a little after these two, so you can either skip forward or skim the fiction section for your own interest and curiosity. I do think that, for certain kinds of non-fiction, fiction building blocks can be useful. If you're writing a narrative story about a true crime case or what have you, you will find some of these principles of value to you.

Who is your main character?

You may well have multiple main characters in your novel, so this applies to them, too. Take some time to consider who is going on this adventure you have planned.

While you're building these characters, you don't need to know everything about them. That comes later. For now, think about the essential elements of them: their values, their goals, and their relationship to the plot.

Your main character is, however, the lens through which we experience the story, for the most part. They are going to be the focal point of the narrative, which means this choice matters. How different would *The Lord of the Rings* have been if told from the perspective of Gimli or Aragorn? The events might have been the same, but their experiences would have colored the narrative, giving it a rather different flavor than it did with Frodo being the main character of the series. (Though a compelling argument could be made for Bill the Pony. Just saying.)

Who is your antagonist?

Just like with the last one, you'll want to consider who, or what, is the force working against your main character. Give them a few attributes and spend a little time writing down your ideas.

Coming up with a general scope of who and what they are is extremely important to the story for obvious reasons. This is true even if the antagonist is something like the ocean itself or the environment, as is the case in books like *Into Thin Air*.

Antagonists are key elements to stories, and without a good antagonist who is constantly driving tension, you end up with a pretty bland tale. The push and pull between the protagonist(s) and antagonist(s) is one of the foundational elements of storytelling. It's like the moon of your plot, affecting the tides you plan to drown your characters in.

What is your central conflict?

Conflict is the defining element of storytelling. *Without conflict, there is no story.* There are no odds to overcome. There is nothing to be achieved or gained. There is just a slice of life without any stakes or payoff. Some genres do lean in this direction, like cozy, but even then, there is tension. The tension may be whether or not Lisa and Alex ever get their tea at the bistro they chose to visit, but it's still some degree of tension.

If a character so much as wants a glass of water and doesn't have one (thanks, Kurt Vonnegut), that's conflict, albeit not particularly *exciting* conflict. Identifying your central conflict will help you move forward with the planning process.

In case you're stumped on this, the central point might be something like:

- A small group of rebels wants to overthrow a tyrannical government (Star Wars)
- A detective has to solve a case and is being hunted by people who very much don't want him solving it (most of The Dresden Files)
- A young woman doesn't want to get married to someone dreadful and is seeking a way out (The Princess Bride)

Conflicts also come in several flavors: major and minor. Minor conflicts will be things that come and go, such as wanting a glass of water, needing to escape a sticky situation, or deciding whether or not to kiss the hot vampire. Major conflicts are things that likely will encompass large swaths of the story. Your characters may have internal conflict (e.g., if I kiss the hot vampire, I'll upset the hot werewolf!) or external conflicts (e.g. that evil wizard is going to kill my entire species if I don't stop him).

Choosing the core conflict of your story is going to be related to your protagonist and why the antagonist is the antagonist. It's also going to be shaped by POV, which I will talk about in a minute. If the core conflict is a war between two countries, the people on both sides typically think they're the good guys.

Where is your story taking place?

This could be the start of world building if you're doing a speculative fiction book, or it could be deciding a rough time period and location for any other kind of story. It can even be as simple as "New York City, modern day" or "Medieval China Analogue."

As with the other questions here, you don't need to have everything fully fleshed out yet (and I wouldn't try to do so—it will just end up stressful). Deciding this element will help you with your planning in the next chapter, where we talk about research.

Knowing where and when your story is taking place is also going to shape character values, technology, and other elements. For example, I went with modern day Boston, MA for my fiction series because I know Boston pretty well and love the idea of commonplace magic. The supernatural being the mundane is a fun storytelling element for me, and with me using a place that actually exists in the real world, I didn't need to recreate the wheel to also play with my modern magic urges. I can just write that characters are on Boylston Ave. and folks will know what that means, or they can look it up on a map.

What POV do you want to tell your story in?

While this isn't a story element exactly, it is one of the major bones of your book. Deciding on your POV (or Point Of View) will mean, when you reach the point of starting the actual writing, you will know what style you're going for.

You don't *have* to plan this in advance, but it certainly helps. Different POV styles create different feels for narration, and they definitely have an impact on the overall storytelling. Knowing what you're going to use before you start writing can be helpful. Deciding it may involve writing a test scene or two and playing with it.

The perspective you tell your story from has a massive impact on the story itself. I point again toward deciding if Frodo, Gimli, or Aragorn should be the main character of *The Lord of the Rings*. Heck, even Sauron. If we experienced a story differently, what might change?

A fun exercise in this might be to consider some of your favorite media and choose another character to center the narrative on. What would it be like to be Amenadiel from *Lucifer*? If we learned the story from his perspective, what would change? What if we were experiencing *Star Wars* from the perspective of a Storm Trooper whose family was saved by the empire driving out crime on his home planet?

These questions can really help you shape your narrative and give you a strong place to begin writing from. If you know why you choose this perspective to write from, you can craft a deeper, richer narrative. Of course, the reason you choose the character doesn't have to be complex. It might just be as simple as, "I like the cut of his jib."

Why do this first?

Even if you're a discovery writer, or a "pantser", you need to have at least a *few* elements of your story in mind before you start writing. Otherwise, you end up almost immediately doomed to get stuck somewhere in the middle. Or you write a lot of gibberish before you settle on anything. At that point, you'll be stuck in rewrites until the apocalypse happens, and you'll probably welcome it. *Ask me how I know.*

What we are doing here is designing a rough idea of what it is we're going to build in our minds. We might not have all the steps labeled out and neat, but we do need to at least know what we are making.

Using Legos as an example, if you start building a castle, then decide to build a rocket ship and finally go with a house, your structure is going to look, uh... interesting. And it *definitely* won't be functional, even for Lego people. Everything might be awesome, but there's only so far you can go with a castle rocket ship house. And by "only so far," I mean "full of building code violations and probably on fire."

It's also okay if the story you end up telling is not the one you planned out in your head. More than once, I have had stories take a hard left turn while I was writing them. In fact, I'd say that happens more frequently than it doesn't. Characters seem to have a mind of their own at times, and we have to hang on for the ride because, well, *here we go.*

Planning Base Elements (Non-Fiction)

Non-fiction is, by nature, a different creature than fiction. Narrative structure and so on will be beneficial for you non-fiction writers to understand, but your core elements are going to differ from fiction in a few ways. Let's take a look at those core elements together, and you can answer the questions for your own work.

What is your core idea?

In non-fiction, you may be telling a narrative (memoir) or not (how-to), but you still have a core concept you would like to convey. This core concept you are working on explaining or discussing is sort of like your "main character" in the sense that it's going to be the thing your book is about.

Unlike with fiction, folks writing non-fiction often know exactly what they want to write about, though some sub-genres get stickier (I mention memoir again). The key to non-fiction, however, is to connect with your readers through sharing something they find useful, interesting, informative, or entertaining.

Since I've been leaning on them a little, memoir writers, for you, this may mean understanding what the goal of your memoir is. Very few people just want to read about the day-to-day life of a person they don't know. If you are telling the story of your life or someone else's, what elements of that story are the interesting ones? Why are you telling it? Is it a story of someone overcoming incredible hardships? Is it a story of someone who experienced a specific kind of trauma, like addiction, for example? Is it about a true crime event? Is it trying to shed light on the experiences of a disadvantaged group of some kind? Those are things you will want to consider as you identify your core purpose in writing this book.

What are you solving for your reader?

With non-fiction, you again are typically trying to address a problem someone has and share information about that problem. The problem might be "doesn't know enough about the Roman Empire," but it's *still* a problem.

In this book, for example, I am addressing people who want to get their books finished and out of their lives. Many better writers than I have published exceptional books on craft. This isn't about craft as much as it is about getting the thing done and out of your brain.

For a book on yoga, the problem might be someone who needs help with wellness or flexibility. For a book on kite flying, the problem might be not knowing where to start. Whatever your subject is, considering how you are going to enrich your reader's life is going to guide you into the process of writing this book.

What credentials do you have to write this book?

Indeed, why *you*? This is something your readers may want to know the answer to, which is why in books like this one, the introduction typically lists the author's credentials and explains why in the heck you'd listen to *them* on this subject.

Think about this as you write, too. While impostor syndrome can, and will, creep in, you should sit for a while and consider the things that make you the best person for this job. If you aren't the best person for this job, why are you doing it?

In terms of this in my personal writing, I am in a rare position as someone who is an author, editor, and who owned a publishing company. There aren't that many editors I know who have done as much as I have in terms of all the different jobs involved in getting a book from idea to print themselves or done it for other people. I also have experience in teaching between coaching authors in various arenas, many years of teaching violin, and a number of years teaching martial arts of various kinds.

So why me? Because I have the knowledge and experience to write a book like this (and its partner, *How to Publish the Damn Book*) and a desire to share everything I know because I'm autistic, and info-dumping is my love language. This gives me the opportunity to do so at length without being the most tedious person at the dinner party.

Who am I writing this book for?

I am going to dig deeper into target audiences in *How to Publish the Damn Book*, but for non-fiction writers, knowing your audience up front is extremely important. If you are writing a how-to guide like this one, you'll want to think about who you're writing for. Are you writing for beginners? Intermediates? Experts looking to polish their game?

Your audience is going to determine a large portion of what you put into your book and how you approach certain topics. For example, if your book is for newbies with no experience, you will want to take care to ensure the beginning steps are laid out thoroughly and not glazed over. However, if your book is for experts, you can presume they know a whole lot more and won't need to rehash the basics. You can also use jargon without explaining it, most likely.

How will this book improve the lives of my readers?

This last question is along similar lines to "what are you solving for your reader" but comes at it from a different angle. Knowing your strategy for how you are going to solve the problem your reader has is going to position you in a far stronger place to know what information to include in your work.

I started this book knowing I wanted to help writers bust through a number of difficult areas of the writing process and get their works out of their brains and onto the page. How I'm doing that is by giving you a bunch of information, including step-by-step instructions in a few areas, and offering you a full tool belt for approaching the process of writing a book.

In order to answer this question, though, you need to know the answers to all the previous questions, which is why this one is at the end. Knowing your core idea and what problem you're addressing is only going to get you so far until you know *who* you are solving that issue for since it changes the angle of approach in many ways.

The most obvious, of course, is that identifying your audience means you'll know how much detail of which parts to include. If it's a memoir, you may be improving the lives of your audience by introducing them to perspectives they may never have experienced before. You also may be improving their life by giving validation to some of the folks who might feel unseen. Reading books by and about disabled people, for example, can help folks feel less alone in their experiences. Non-disabled people may learn more about disability and become more empathetic. These questions are going guide you as you move forward.

Plotter vs. Discovery Writer

As promised, I'm going to get into the divide between "plotters" and "discovery writers." A lot of people will have you believe there are two camps or that there are even other types of writers, but I think a lot of this is a fallacy. While, yes, some writers like to plan their books out far more than others, I think everybody is a mix of both. I say this as an autistic planner who has a 20+ book series laid out in Plottr right now. Staring at me. Waiting.

And I am ignoring it to write *this* book instead. You're welcome. (Don't make eye contact with your unfinished drafts. They gain power that way.)

Whether you lean toward having everything meticulously planned in advance or like to discover things as you go, there's no "wrong" way of writing a book with the exception of any technique that doesn't lead you to a finished product. If you try a method and cannot write that way, well... obviously, that's wrong for you. It's similar to fashion. Some people can pull off looks that the rest of us look ridiculous in.

Every writer's needs, and every book's needs, are different. Some stories don't really need excessive plotting because they don't have a lot of twists, side stories, foreshadowing, things to remember from book one that surface in book twelve, and so on. How complex a story is, how many moving parts there are, how big the series is, and how you as an author think is going to determine how much plotting in advance you need to do.

The artificial divide of "plotter" and "discovery writer" just creates static where there doesn't really need to be any. If an author cannot seem to finish a book for the life of them and keeps getting hung up in the middle? Well, there's a good chance that they didn't do enough planning. If an author can't ever seem to get started because their outline isn't *just so*, they probably are doing too much planning. Where that happy middle ground is, is all about your unique, personal needs and your book's requirements. Full stop.

It also may change. If you go from writing a very light standalone story that's straightforward without intense, complex world building to writing something like *The Wheel of Time*? Chances are your needs are going to shift from not having to do much planning to needing to do a whole lot of it.

Just as with many elements of the writing process, you will discover your needs may change over time and depend on the story and genre you are working in. I also am of the opinion that the more experienced you are, the less of certain types of planning you might find yourself needing to do.

As you learn the shape of narrative, the craft of writing, your genre, and your own needs, you may discover you can plan a little less and rely on your instincts a little more. That said, with a *Wheel of Time*-style narrative, you will need to do a *lot* of certain kinds of planning no matter what, and you had best have your series bible handy because you're gonna need it.

The Principle of Outlines

Okay, remember when I told you I'd warn you when you could run screaming if you don't intend on writing an outline? This is that point. I still hope you won't, though. Because even if you don't intend on writing the kind of outline we learned in high school English, there are things in here that might be helpful for you. That said, if you want to flee, I validate your choices and will see you in chapter two.

Outlining is actually a far larger and broader set of methods than what we learned for papers in school, and that method often hurts creatives because it takes things down to a level that's far too granular. While some folks really like that, and I'm not going to tell them they're wrong, I feel like it doesn't leave me with enough creative energy by the time I'm done with the outline to write the rest of the book.

That is, I believe, the thing that draws writers away from outlining: that feeling that they're pouring all their creative energy into writing the outline and subsequently losing excitement for the book itself. It's a feeling I completely understand if you're trying to outline the way we learned in school. Is that method worthless? No. It's actually how I wrote this book. However, that particular method is best suited for *non-fiction*. After all, fiction rarely comes with a thesis statement.

Blake Snyder's Beat Sheet (out of his book *Save the Cat*) is the best outlining method I've ever found. However, it's not the only method. I actually combine it with elements of *The Snowflake Method* pioneered by Randy Ingermanson. These two things smooshed together really make the most sense to me. While I encourage you to research both those methods—after you're done reading *this* most excellent book, of course—the principle I am suggesting is this:

Whatever storytelling method you choose, I suggest you plan out the major story events. Whether you use the Beat Sheet or the broad strokes pieces I advised in the last chapter or some other method I haven't read about, write down a collection of significant events in the story based on the major pinch points. If nothing else, you should develop a plan for the opening, the catalyst, the midpoint, the finale, and the ending. Even if you do no other outlining and planning, if you have each of those five elements in your head, you will know the next thing you're working on.

That's really the value of an outline.

How much further detail you get into and how granular you get with your planning after those five elements is a function of taste and how complex the story is. But if you have those elements, you will have a solid roadmap for about each fifth of the book, and you'll know what you're building toward.

When authors get stuck partway through their manuscript, the most common reason for that is they don't know what their next major story element is supposed to be. And when they don't know that, they don't know how to get there *because they don't even know where they're going*.

I always liken an outline to a map for a road trip. Some people like to plan out every stop, but even if you don't plot out every single turn (and leave yourself room to turn off the highway to see the World's Biggest Ear of Corn), it's best to know a few points along the route to ensure you are even going to make it to your eventual destination. If you have no destination and no plans whatsoever, there's a really good chance you won't get where you're going because you're not actually *going* anywhere.

This may feel a bit loud to folks who are discovery writers, and I promise I'm not trying to square up with you (assuming you're still here). However, that struggle is the reason why the vast majority of discovery writers I know struggle with act two (I favor the three-act structure, so when I reference acts, that's usually what I mean). Act two is actually *half the dang book*. From the catalyst to the finale is a solid fifty percent of your word count, and if you don't have anything planned for that 30,000-50,000 words of your story, you're not going to have a fun time writing it.

It is for this reason I advise people to plan at least the five plot points I have above. It's also why I like using the Beat Sheet to plan out the broad strokes of my story. It means I have far fewer words to figure out between plot points if I'm playing *Connect The Dots*™ with my manuscript. Planning out those essential elements provides me with sufficient direction without limiting me by deciding *how* I get between those elements. (Or visiting the World's Largest Ear of Corn.)

Idea Generation and Planning

Of course, this also has the added benefit of not writing my story before I write my story. Maybe it's the eternal battle between my ADHD and autism in my brain, but I absolutely need a combination of structure and freedom. Parameters are important.

This may seem like a sudden subject change, but I promise it's not.

I am a musician. I've played violin since I was six years old and started learning music at age four when I began piano lessons. Having the basic elements in place is like deciding what time signature and key you are composing in as well as maybe identifying a few key chord changes.

However, I can improvise the melody all over those chords and use all sorts of interesting rhythms over that time signature. I am not *limited* by those foundation elements of the piece. I am guided and given direction but not constrained.

Also, you can change keys and time signatures in a piece if you want to. That's a thing.

Outlines are similar: They provide a few guideposts and elements of the story, but whether you write every note in advance or freestyle it based on the principles you created, it's all about how you approach the piece as an individual artist.

Summary

In this chapter, we discussed the early planning stages of preparing your book. This includes figuring out where ideas come from and busting a few myths about that, how to do some basic planning for fiction and non-fiction, and going through the difference between a plotter and a discovery writer (or pantser).

Hopefully at this point, you have a mental image of where you can start your process of writing!

Key Takeaways

- You don't need to write a "unique" story—you have to write your story.
- Using media and other sources for inspiration is a tried and true method of coming up with ideas for your book.
- You should spend time consuming media in the genre(s) you want to work in and use that to study the expected tropes and needs of the readers of that media.
- Work on how you engage with media. Start thinking critically about the works you consume and look at them as opportunities to study your craft.
- Don't ask for feedback too early or else you will end up overwhelmed and feeling as though you have been kicked.
- Consider the core elements of your type of writing (fiction or non-fiction) and answer the questions laid out in those segments as you start preparing to write.
- Plotters and discovery writers are just separate sliders on a spectrum that can run the gamut between the two. The only wrong answer is the one that doesn't work for you.
- Outlines are very important tools for writers, even if you are a discovery writer. Whether you write one before you start writing or make notes as you go, they are valuable!

Chapter Two

Story Craft and the Star Point Method

Being autistic, one of my many strengths is in pattern recognition. One of the things I have noticed as I have studied story structure through the years is that most story structure methods used in the West (not including indigenous storytelling about which I am not informed enough to have an opinion) have a very similar pattern of rising and falling tension.

This pattern made itself clear to me when I was planning a talk on something entirely different for the first Neurodivergent Publishing Conference in 2023. Naturally, I pivoted my entire talk and made slides at 3 a.m., thus bringing the Star Point Method into being.

Out of this pattern, I have developed my own story crafting method based on that push and pull of tension, which is what I maintain is the core piece of any story. The tug and release on your reader's heart and mind is going to produce works people struggle to put down, and mastering that art will put you in a powerful position to capture people's attention, interest, and fandom.

While this definitely *does* fall a little deeper into the craft segment of things than I plan to dig into in this book, I feel this is important enough to the ability to get the story out and written that taking some time to discuss story structure is going to be of significant help to people trying to figure out their plot.

The Function of Tension

By its nature, most (Western) fictional narratives tend to follow a very similar pattern of rising and falling action. Regardless of what you call the structure (three-act structure, five-act structure, hero's journey, etc.), the pattern of rising and falling tension is almost universal. I say almost because some indigenous storytelling narrative forms do *not* follow those methods whatsoever. Those types are just as valid as the ones with which I am familiar, but I profess that I am not anywhere near as knowledgeable about them to do them justice, so the best I can do here is acknowledge their existence and validity. As with most things writing-related, there is no "One True Way." However, the pattern I'm going to explain to you and the information I'm setting forth in this chapter is going to be one of the proven effective methods out there.

This structure of storytelling is explained in a million and one ways, but most of them have very similar elements broken down in different ways. My personal favorite is Blake Snyder's "Beat Sheet" from his book *Save the Cat*. I can, and often do, expound on it at length, but instead of me rehashing what Mr. Snyder has already done, I am more inclined to tell you to pick up a copy of *Save the Cat* and/or *Save the Cat Writes a Novel* by Jessica Brody. After you're done with this one, of course.

Another thing tension plays into is a word you'll hear a lot when discussing story craft: conflict. I'll explain a little more about that later on in this section, but keep it in your mind.

There are many ways to use tension in a novel, and I firmly believe that mastering the art of utilizing tension in storytelling is one of the most important things a writer can learn about story craft. Before we get too deep into the pattern of rising and falling tension, however, I want to dig a little into the two main types of tension you can have in your book and how to deploy them.

Internal Tension

This is, as you may imagine, conflict that occurs inside the character. Tension of this type can be relatively short (e.g., deciding what shirt to wear between two options) or run the length of a novel or series (e.g., Anikin Skywalker struggling with the Dark Side). The depth of this conflict and the importance of it will shape not only the character but that character's relationship with the entire world beyond their head.

To get a little personal here, I have CPTSD caused by prolonged childhood trauma. I experience a great deal of internal tension when one of my triggers is hit. I have an immediate emotional reaction and have to manually remind myself I am not in that situation anymore. That takes time to handle and colors my interactions with certain people and certain experiences in the world. That is one example of internal tension that is long-term.

A short-term internal tension might be me trying to decide what the hell to eat for lunch. (Send help. I don't know today, either.) This can either be a manifestation of a person being over-tired, overstimulated, over-stressed, or might just be an example of an indecisive character struggling to make choices. All of those can be small pieces of internal tension that add up to something bigger.

Internal tension can be reflected in many ways through how a character acts, and that character's personal struggle might be the basis for their entire arc. (I'm looking at you, Prince Zuko.) As a result, this kind of tension frequently drives character development.

Character-driven stories are ones in which the character's growth and change over the course of the plot are considered intrinsic to the storytelling. These stories typically feature characters whose heads we are in (or closer to) and share emotional journeys that see the character develop and change substantially from the beginning of the story through to the end.

Examples of character-driven media include works like *Shawshank Redemption*, the *Dresden Files* books, *Avatar: the Last Airbender*, and the TV series *Firefly*.

External Tension

External tension is likely to come in the form of events or situations the character has no control over. It might be a war in their country, or it might be a snowstorm making travel difficult. As the name implies, it's the stress of being acted upon by forces beyond oneself.

Using this kind of tension to put characters into situations where they need to react is one of the elements that typically drives plot. Plot-focused books are often full of this kind of event because the story is more about what's happening than about what it's doing to the characters interacting with it.

Think about it—action movie heroes rarely have to deal with PTSD or disability following their injuries. The fact that Tony Stark from the Marvel movies and comics displayed obvious signs of PTSD in *Iron Man 3* was honestly one of the first times I have memory of a character in an action franchise showing it on the big screen.

That's not to say there's anything wrong with plot-driven stories. There isn't. However, external tension alone is going to be one of those things that drives a plot-driven story versus a character-driven story.

Examples of stories like these are things like the *James Bond* movies, *Ready Player One*, *The Da Vinci Code*, and *Jurassic Park*.

Using Both

A good story, no matter what the medium is, will have a mix of plot-driven elements and character-driven elements. Very few works of any merit at all are exclusively one or the other, though I won't claim it's *impossible*. The key is creating a good balance between the two. They can also play into one another. External tension can create internal tension, and internal tension can manifest in external tension.

For example, let's say there's a character who has magic powers associated with their emotions. If they have an emotional meltdown on a ship while they and others are traveling, perhaps they create a massive storm. The storm could be a point of external tension that is caused by the character's internal chaos. Moments like that are not uncommon in media.

To use a less magical example, if a soldier on a battlefield has a crisis of conscience and has important battle plans, say they defect to the enemy and share those battle plans. Their internal crisis results in the tide of the war changing and causes external tension for other characters.

Going the other direction, being in a war would cause anybody to have emotional difficulties and could cause a great deal of internal crisis. It does so regularly to real, living humans. So do things like earthquakes and massive storms. Or, say, a virus spreading around the entire planet killing millions of people and disrupting the entire world's ability to function. (COVID, anyone?) PTSD due to those catastrophes is a natural, human response.

Tension and Conflict

Conflict causes tension; tension causes conflict. These two ideas are consistently interlocked in the writing sphere, but many people misunderstand the relationship. All conflict *does* cause tension, and tension can be both the product of a conflict and the source of that conflict at the same time.

As I mentioned earlier, the stakes don't need to be extremely high for these two concepts to appear in your book. The conflict of will two characters date or not causes romantic tension. The conflict of a character trying to decide whether or not they want to kiss the romantic lead can cause an increase of tension before they actually seal the deal.

As you will learn, conflict is the core driving force of a book. It's the thing that's at the core of the entire narrative. That conflict can be as simple as wanting a romantic partner but not being sure if the lead is ready for one, or it can be as complex and nuanced as a war on a massive scale with all the shades of gray in between.

The way I view the relationship of conflict and tension is the two cause one another like some kind of strange Ouroboros. They are separate things, but they are deeply related. The best way I can describe it is that conflict is like of two pieces of stone grinding against one another, whereas the heat and dust and friction are the tension. The tension there is what's making the stones grind rather than glide, but the stones moving against one another produces the friction.

Throughout the story, there will be many small conflicts as well as multiple, much larger ones. That's the nature of storytelling and of life.

The Points of the Star

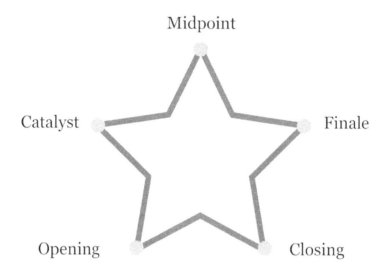

When it comes to storytelling, your plot is going to be built on the core of the push/pull of tension through the story. This tug and release builds the tension in your stories, has a direct relationship with pacing, and is the closest thing we authors have to "secret sauce" when it comes to what it is that keeps readers coming back over and over again.

As I've mentioned a few times, tension doesn't need to come with world-altering consequences in order to be important to the characters. In a romance, the tension is often about whether or not the characters will be able to fall in love or stick it out through whatever difficulties the plot throws at them. The whole world won't end if they don't end up dating (typically).

This push/pull pattern is actually how I came up with the name "Star Point Method." The increase of tension creates a "point" with a trough between. Since there are five major tension points, our pattern of rising and falling tension can look an awful lot like a classic "star" shape.

However.

Between those five main points, which I will get into shortly, you can add smaller points of tension. This can create an almost fractal effect of moments of push and pull which, again, looks very much like a star. The balance of push and release is really the key here. That's what makes up this method.

Without further ado, let's get into the five "points" of the Star Point Method.

The Opening

At the very beginning, tension is low. While yes, you can start *in media res* and begin with a bang, that's not quite what I mean here. The thing that draws the character into the main, overarching plot shouldn't usually happen in the first scene.

The job of your first chapter(s) is establishing your setting and your characters in the world as they know it before whatever event drags them, kicking and screaming, into the story. I say "kicking and screaming" because the catalyst often involves bad things happening to people. Even if the inciting event *is* a good thing, it's often a bad one. They just don't know it yet. See? Tension!

As a general rule, the opening part of a book should start with something to grab a reader's attention (the "hook") and then can relax a little into some of the setting stuff. That hook is the first major point of tension in the story.

The Catalyst

Speaking of inciting events, the second point of our star is our catalyst—the thing that draws your main character(s) into the story and really gets things rolling. It's the second major hit of tension in the story. Your catalyst should be pretty high stakes because otherwise, why would the story matter or the characters bother?

Now, "high stakes" doesn't have to mean saving the world, though it can. It could be something as simple as needing to find a new job so they don't lose their apartment. Maybe they break up with a partner. Maybe they learn an asteroid is about to destroy their home planet. Regardless of what the inciting event is, it is a big point of strain in the character's life and drags them out of their life before and thrusts them into the world of the story.

The inciting event's conclusion and the character(s) beginning the main part of the story is also the starting point for act two, whether you're using the three-act or five-act structure. This means you're poised to launch the characters into their mission, whatever that mission may be.

This moment should be higher tension than your opening since it's going to be the first time the character really hits the main plot of the book. However, after that initial tension, you'll be letting off the gas a little to give readers a chance to breathe and the character, the opportunity to orient to their new situation. This doesn't mean to make it boring, of course. Also, after that release, you'll want to start ratcheting things up because the next point of our star is going to be the highest point of tension in the story. If you go from zero to a hundred, you'll give readers unpleasant whiplash.

The Midpoint

In all the various story structures out there used to describe Western storytelling, *this is where tension is the highest.* This moment, usually in the middle of the story in terms of both word count and narrative, encapsulates the time when the tension is at a fever pitch. It doesn't matter what genre or what story it is, this is where things are ready to explode. And of course, they do. That explosion happens immediately after the midpoint. Think of this as that moment when you're blowing a bubble with chewing gum, and you know the bubble has reached critical mass. You're hoping it doesn't burst and get in your hair, but it's too far along now to stop because you're *committed.*

This point of tension might look like everything in the character's life appearing to be wonderful and secretly falling out from underneath them *or* it could appear that everything is about as horrible as it's going to get.

After the midpoint, you have a space between there and the finale where characters are going to wrestle with what happened at the midpoint and deal with the consequences of that part of the story. It is also the point of the story where things often feel hopeless for the characters. The lovers will never get together; the bad guys are winning after a major blow... Whatever happened at the midpoint, the "lull" before the finale is the characters handling that.

The Finale

This is, of course, when the characters rally again after everything goes wrong and enact whatever plan they came up with as a solution. The tension here should be very high, but not quite as high as the midpoint. However, we need to keep readers engaged, so don't drop the tension too low just yet.

I know many of the visual aids of novels have the tension go down as quickly as it rose (Freytag's Pyramid, I'm looking at you, just so you know). That's not the best visualization because it implies that the final confrontation has less tension than the previous two segments of the story, and that just isn't the case.

This is the big push when the narrative is hitting that "Ahah!" moment, and the characters are launching their final salvo on whatever the antagonist of the story is. Depending on the genre, they may or may not be successful in this attempt, but it is the big moment of giving it their all after being badly beaten up by the events of the midpoint and what comes after.

The Closing

Regardless of whether the final confrontation goes well or poorly, the conclusion of the book should conclude with a drop in tension. It is, however, worth noting that books that are part of a series should end with more tension than books that have no intended sequels. If you are ending a book and closing it all up with a bow, there's no need to retain tension here. However, if you're working in a series, you'll want to leave some tension here to keep people wanting the next book. While the main plot should be entirely wrapped up by that point, there ought to be something to carry readers into the next one.

I also *strongly* advise against cliffhangers unless you are doing a rapid-release strategy or have the second book written and ready to go within a year or so because doing that to readers is going to get you a lot of *feels*. If something happens, and you never conclude the story, it's the literary equivalent of leaving a partner unsatisfied in bed, and we don't want to do that to our readers. After all, if you do that to folks, people don't come back for seconds.

Using the Points

If you understand these five moments in your story structure and know when, where, and how they enter your manuscript, you will be able to write a story that readers want to finish reading, *and* you'll save yourself a lot of trouble wandering around in the weeds trying to figure out what happens next.

This won't prevent you from getting hung up at every point, but it can certainly help you identify what your next major plot element is and give you a direction to run in. Understanding the pattern a story follows is one of the big literary keys. It's the "secret sauce" that makes your novel flow from one chapter to the next. 'It's also one of the things that makes readers come back again and again. There's a reason Hollywood uses the same pattern of rising and falling tension. The major writers do, too.

Using the Star Point Method is as simple as writing out the five points on some notebook paper (or typing it on your PC, but I'm old fashioned) and then noting down what you want to have happen at those points.

As I mentioned at the outset to this segment, you can easily add as many "points" to your star as you feel your story needs. This method is adaptable for many different authors, and you can make it work with your brain. For discovery writers, you might just have a few words or a single sentence at each point. For plotters, you might need to write down every single event along the timeline between the points. There is no wrong way to do this except the one that doesn't work for you.

My reason for providing such a loose structure is multi-faceted, to be honest. The first is that many story structures are viewed as highly rigid and not to be altered. That means those folks might end up writing stories that have no breathing room to them and come out very similar to one another in shape. It's not healthy to force something into a shape it's not meant to take.

Secondly, this method is adaptable. My main struggle with so many of the story structures out there is that they are either too much or not enough. The ones that are too much overwhelm people who just don't plan stories out like that and ones that aren't enough offer insufficient guidance for how to get from point to point.

The last reason for it is, honestly, that this method makes the most sense to me. The whole key to this thing isn't the points themselves but the relationship they have to one another. If you ignore the dip in tension between them, you end up with a pentagon, not a star. The shape of the tension (dropping between the points while rising or lowering over all prior to the midpoint) is one of the most necessary pieces here.

The way these points interact with one another and the space between them is the entire ball of wax. Creating that feeling of push and pull is the core to developing tension that keeps readers coming back. If you get the tension correct, people will gravitate to your writing, even if they don't know precisely why.

Summary

In this chapter, we've talked about tension and conflict and their role in storytelling. We've also covered my method for story planning, the Star Point Method. Understanding the way tension will push and pull characters through the story and how those pieces interact with one another will give you a strong base for ensuring your story remains gripping for readers.

Key Takeaways

- Tension can be broken down into two categories: internal and external. These categories are both important to stories.
- Tension and conflict are different things but are both integral to the story.
- Tension rises and falls throughout the course of the story in a measurable pattern for most works using Western storytelling techniques.
- This pattern of rising and falling tension can be used to help you know when and where in your story to have certain events happen, and can help you keep your plot driving forward even as you release tension to give readers a chance to catch their breath.

Chapter Three

Researching For Your Book

Research is one of those topics that brings out one of two reactions in people: wide-eyed glee or the desire to howl at the moon in frustration. You might well end up with a mix of both those feelings at some point during the process, too. It's definitely not an either/or sort of situation. This chapter is designed to help you identify things that you *must* research so you don't miss anything important, as well as how to do the process at all since research is difficult these days.

Research in general is a skill that often falls by the wayside in modern education, and it's a challenging one. I like to joke that I essentially got a degree in research (I have a B.A. in European history) because I spent a lot of time learning how to find information and how to suss out resources that are good and how to evaluate sources critically. I'm going to get into some of that in further segments of this chapter, but I do want to note that doing so is of utmost importance. Some subjects naturally require less critical thinking than others (if you Google the capital of Alabama, for example, you are unlikely to get conflicting answers), but not everything you might need to study as an author will be so cut and dry.

With the invention of the internet, research in and of itself is both easier and harder than ever before. I come from that weird middle generation who both did library research using microfiche as well as witnessing the dawn of the mighty Wikipedia. Between elementary school and college, it went from card catalogs to Google, and I've seen both sides of that coin. There are benefits and drawbacks to both, and while I'm not able to give you an entire course on research methods here, I'll do my best to share what I think will be the most useful principles for authors.

Also, since I feel this needs to be addressed, do not use ChatGPT or other AI engines for researching. At the time of writing this, they tend to hallucinate badly and often, so any information coming out of them will have to be verified to the point that you will be better off doing the research yourself from whole cloth.

I don't hate AI's existence, and I find it useful for a great many things, but there's no place for it in research at this point in time.

What You Need to Research

We all know there are people who will be very upset if you get elements of your story wrong (I'm a history nerd; we get *salty*), but we can't know everything. We're here to create stories, not write manuals. Knowing how to approach research, what you absolutely need to research, and what you can mostly ignore, is a core skill.

So, what are things you're going to need to actually do research on when writing? I can't give you every single subject you're going to need to know about since every book requires different types and levels of research. However, I can give you some broad strokes categories.

Cultures that are not your own

Seriously, **if you research literally nothing else in the course of writing your book, study this.** If you are going to write about people from cultures of which you are not a part, study those cultures. By culture, I don't necessarily mean nationality, either. The United States (where I live) has hundreds, if not thousands, of subcultures based on nationality, religious affiliation, political philosophy, geographic location, gender, sexuality, amount of money one was born with, profession, and about a million other things.

I'm not going to discourage someone from writing about a culture that isn't their own, but I will say that if re going to do it, do it in a way that shows you did your ___ to understand them.

Failure to do so will, at best, result in eye rolling from people in that subculture. At worst, you can perpetuate harmful stereotypes about folks who have been hurt enough already.

As a person who is part of several marginalized groups—physically disabled, neurodivergent (twice exceptional), non-binary, queer—I can say with certainty that many of the stereotypes I have seen about people like myself cause real harm. Up to and including the fact that my neurodivergence was undiagnosed, and I struggled to get a diagnosis for my Ehlers-Danlos Syndrome because doctors assumed that I was "just" anxious, depressed, and making it up. No, it turns out I have a genetic disorder that makes my joints slipperier than black ice on the highway.

I'm also late-diagnosed autistic, not broken. I have ADHD; I'm not lazy. I'm disabled; I don't lack a work ethic. I'm pansexual, not "confused." I'm non-binary, not "confused."

If I sound bitter about those things, it's because I am. Those kinds of stereotypes really do hurt people and have more cultural impact than you might imagine. Doing your research in good faith will help you avoid doing more harm to people who don't deserve it.

Technology in your book's time period

When I say "technology" here, I mean more than cell phones and computers. As I mentioned earlier on, I am a historian, and I cannot tell you the number of times I've been reading a "historical" novel and come across a character wearing jeans or a T-shirt, at which point I throw the book. Or mime throwing my Kindle because that thing is expensive and I am *not* chucking it across the room, but the sentiment is there.

If you're building a fantasy setting, you're not inherently bound by the rules of our world. That is absolutely true, but too many people use that as a cop out to avoid doing research. That's how we end up with elf kings in jeans and a tunic while wielding a sword and crossbow. You do not need to be an actual historian (though it helps if you know one who can beta read for you) or a scientist if we're talking sci-fi, but make sure you do your best to study the time period.

And *don't* do that by watching movies. In particular, don't do it by watching *Gladiator*. That movie's title alone is enough to make every history nerd in the world scream in fury all at once, even if we only do it in our heads. Movies often get historical details incredibly wrong. I don't mean things like alternative history, where someone is creating a narrative out of something that could've happened. I mean things like their portrayal of the medieval period as grubby, drab, and universally unwashed. None of those things were true. Medieval people, even peasants, wore vibrant clothing, bathed regularly, and tried to stay clean and neat where possible. Certain places like cities often had areas of squalor, but that's not so different from today. That doesn't mean nobody bathed.

How injuries you inflict on your characters really work

While I am using this space to vent a bit of a pet peeve of mine, this is something writers really should do some more study on. Unfortunately, action movies have led us all to believe that being shot should only matter to a body when it's dramatic, and that being shot or stabbed in the shoulder is a nothing injury. Also, things like grazes are easily ignored, and soldiers can ignore all pain forever and never cry for their mothers.

None of those things are true.

One of my very best friends, author Leslie E. Heath, was an ER nurse for many years, and I frequently ask her questions about things I do to my characters. Fortunately, she's also a writer and hasn't reported me to the FBI (yet). If you are going to inflict bodily injury on your characters, doing some internet searching will tell you a lot about what the kind of injury does. There are also books out there on the subject, such as *Body Trauma* by David W. Page, MD, FACS. If that's something you are going to be dealing with in your writing, I cannot suggest highly enough that you learn more about it.

How mental illnesses really present

Much in line with the first thing on this list, if you are dealing with mental illness in your book and do not have that particular struggle yourself, you should study it. This may mean talking to a psychologist or psychiatrist about it, reading the DSM-V or whatever version is out when you are reading this, and coming to understand it.

This particular point is something that is deeply personal to me because I have CPTSD in addition to my ADHD and autism (which are not a mental illnesses, I know). I have also often seen people with my particular issues portrayed in ways that are not genuine and either infantilize people with my conditions, particularly the autism and ADHD, or miss the mark entirely and misunderstand what the condition is like to live with (CPTSD).

I also have friends who are schizophrenic, have Down's Syndrome, and many other mental challenges of various kinds. They are so often portrayed badly in the media, which only serves to increase stigma. As I write this, it's 2024, and I am going to take the stance that we are far beyond the point where we should do better.

Weaponry and combat

Again, if this is germane to your story, and you are going to be including this in your book, you really should understand it. You don't need to be an expert, but if you have someone using a rapier like a broadsword, you are going to have all the history nerds groaning. The same is true of firearms. In the next segment about how to gather data, I'll explain more about it, but the easy way around this is to talk to someone who has at least a passing familiarity with the art form you're trying to portray. Either that, or do some YouTube viewing.

Not doing this kind of research will result in both extremely unrealistic combat as well as breaking immersion pretty hard for readers who know anything about it. If you are choosing to write in a more anime-like style where you aren't going to get into the nitty-gritty of combat, that's all right. But you should choose to do so from a position of knowing what reality is before you break the rules.

Well, there you have it. Those are the five areas of writing that I feel authors absolutely *must* research if they are germane to the books they're writing. Not every author needs every one of these elements, but if you are going to include these things in your books, knowing about them is deeply important.

There are, of course, many other things that your book will require you to research. Book three of my *Boston Blight* series necessitated me to do an unreasonable amount of research about sailboats and sailing, as well as CIA lingo, tradecraft, and probably about a dozen things that have me on FBI watch lists. I'm sure of it.

Choosing Your Sources

Getting into the nitty gritty of how to research things could be an entire book unto its own, so I'm going to try and distill the principles of critical research skills down as far as I can to give you a collegiate-level crash course in how to go about looking things up. While I am focusing on primarily internet resources here, the same principles will apply to *all* resources, whether print or virtual. Even if I suggest starting with Wikipedia, you could start with an encyclopedia that was printed, but you'll still need to double-check where the information came from and who gathered it.

It's tempting to feel like print sources are more reliable than internet ones, but the reality is that print sources are subject to the same sorts of errors internet or virtual sources have.

However you want to go about selecting the sources you draw from, do your best. Writers cannot be experts in everything that shows up in our books. We just can't. And if you need to write about something you're not an expert about and can't research well or easily? Leave it vague. Let people's imaginations fill in the gaps. Instead of calling your character's firearm an M&P Shield 9mm, just call it a semi-automatic pistol or, even more vague, a gun. Make and model often doesn't matter that much in the context of a story anyway.

Start with Wikipedia

Despite what we were taught in school, there's nothing wrong with Wikipedia as a starting point. I wouldn't necessarily *end* there, depending on how far down the rabbit hole you go, but if you need general insight into most things, it's a strong start. One of the nice things about Wikipedia, however, is the fact that it links to sources for its material most of the time. That allows you to continue your research in less changeable locations if you are studying something that requires more specified knowledge. However, if you just need to know general details about something like the War of 1812 or general information about King Andrew III of Hungary, you can get enough to go on by using it.

The bad rap Wikipedia has for being editable is also one of its strengths. Information on there is typically up to date, and misinformation (and disinformation) is removed quickly and ruthlessly. While, yes, individual writers may skew to one direction or another when it comes to certain pieces, you run that risk anywhere. Take what you read with a grain of salt, but recognize that the vast majority of its content is excellent and certainly sufficient to use for fiction.

Vet your sources (when it matters).

On the internet, nobody knows you're a cat. No, seriously. What I mean by that is that when you are researching, you are going to run into websites, articles, and sources you're going to need to vet. For example, while working on book three of *Boston Blight*, I needed to study CIA tradecraft. Basically, spy stuff. The CIA, of course, is notoriously tight-lipped about what they do, so finding actual information is challenging unless you know somebody. And even if you do, they might not talk to you about it. In fact, they probably won't.

As a result, I had to do a lot of studying to find out certain elements of how a CIA operator would actually do things. For example, did you know that in America, they're not called "agents?" They never have been. That's a British thing. They're called operators, operatives, or officers, most of the time.

There, now you're on a watch list, too. HAH!

In order to find that information, I went down a rabbit hole that led me to something that came off Wikileaks. Now, that site is dubious at best, so everything on there needed to be taken with an entire shaker of salt. However, when I found the document, I immediately started cross referencing it with things I had already learned, talked to some folks I know who know more than I do, and guessed that the contents of the document were at least close enough to real for me to adopt the terminology into my writing.

This was all a very roundabout way to show my method of evaluating, but it comes down to being able to corroborate the data elsewhere on reliable sources. *Reliable* being the key. Reliable sources tend to include things like government websites, industry journals for things like the sciences, history, archaeology, etc., major news outlets (again, you're looking for the data they all show, not just things one of them does), individuals with specific knowledge of a location (like the curator of a museum), or industry experts.

Finally, when dealing with opinions, one of the most important things you can do is check the source itself. If you find an article on a website that isn't one of the major, reliable sources, take a look at the website itself. Read who created it and why. Read about the author of the article. See who benefits from the article being written. If it's a study, see who funded it. If you're looking at a study saying smoking is harmless that's funded by a tobacco company, you can rule that out as non-biased pretty quickly, for example.

Also, you should know when you don't need to double- and triple-check your sources. If you're just looking up information about where a government building is located in a city, you can probably trust the first result with its address unless it's classified or some such. If you want to know when the War of 1812 happened, you can probably trust the first result in Google.

The process of vetting and cross-checking your sources is mostly to be used on things where easy and clear information is less obvious, or the subject is contentious and likely to draw multiple points of view, such as politically charged issues.

Also, for non-fiction, you may need to do a whole lot more of this. Fiction has a lot more loose rules because it's usually about a story, but if you're writing a work of non-fiction, be prepared to be scrutinized pretty hard, particularly in things like politics, true crime, and so on.

Ask people with firsthand experience.

This one might seem obvious, but you'd be amazed how frequently we overlook the power of asking someone directly. I have a very eclectic friend group, and I have had to ask friends questions on everything from Colonial cemetery terminology to emergency medicine. And when you don't have a friend who knows? There are other options!

When you're researching something like sailboats, you don't need to go to the Smithsonian. I asked questions on an online forum (I needed to know about how many miles a boat of a specific size could go on a single tank of gasoline) and talked to a couple people in my life who are very familiar with sailing and do it as a hobby. They definitely knew enough to get me the information I needed. You'd also be amazed at what you can find on Reddit.

Keep in mind that if you are entering a space for people who are really into that specific thing, you should respect those people and thank them for taking the time to answer.

You can also use websites like Quora or even send emails to places directly. For example, I sent an email to the Old North Church asking them specific questions about the church for my novel. I couldn't go there myself thanks to COVID (they weren't doing tours), but I got in touch with someone who led tours of the church and crypt. I also looked at photos of the place and used it as an excuse to boot up *Fallout 4*.

This kind of research can also work really well with things like martial arts. If you have a friend with some training, having them read a fight scene for you can be a great resource in how to clean things up. You could also go to a local martial arts school and ask to watch some spars or talk to the sensei. If you can find a HEMA group in your area, you might be able to watch them have bouts and ask questions of the fighters there about the armor and weapons from people who've handled them.

This also includes things like talking to people who experience a thing you're writing about. If you want to learn more about what it's like to have PTSD, talk to someone who has it. The same could be said of folks of different cultural backgrounds to yourself. When in doubt, go to the source. Of course, no culture or group is a monolith, so recognize that one person's experience may not define what everyone goes through or experiences, but talking to the people who actually live the thing you're trying to write cannot be overstated in its importance and value.

Do the thing (or go the place) yourself.

As much as on-paper research helps when we cannot do the thing, there is no substitute for experience. If you have the ability to try some of the things you're attempting to describe, you will be able to do so with far more authenticity. For example, if you're going to be doing a lot of firearms scenes in your book, it might be a good idea to go to a range with someone and hold, and fire, a comparable weapon.

If you're going to describe a location in your book, you should try and go there yourself if you can. If that isn't possible, you'd be amazed at what kind of feel for a location you can get from Google Maps street view, however. Despite COVID, I was able to stroll around the city of

Boston and explore the location to my heart's content to refresh my memory since I couldn't go there in person at the time.

Even if you are unable to do the exact thing yourself, you might be able to find a local analogue that will give you more of an idea of what it's like. I might not be able to go skydiving, but I certainly can go to an amusement park and ride the biggest, sheerest drop they have and experience the sensation of free fall. It's definitely not the same, but it's close enough that I can describe some of the physical sensations. And of course, it's for research. Ahem. Research!

Obviously, I don't suggest you break the law or put yourself in physical danger to attempt to experience things your characters do. So please don't go get shot, stabbed, run over, or blown up for the sake of authenticity. Please.

How to Organize Your Research

All this research you're doing has to go somewhere, right? So how in the heck do you make it accessible to you while you're writing?

There are a lot of ways, to be honest.

If you don't want to do digital, you can print things out, or take notes, and keep them in a three-ring binder or multi-subject notebook with dividers. You could create a conspiracy theory board with all the red string your strange little heart desires. You could use index cards that you store on your desk. You could write it on your skin with a Sharpie! I don't suggest that one, though. People look at you funny.

When it comes to physical methods, I'm old fashioned and prefer to write things out long hand. I used paper for many years before moving to a Rocketbook and finally to an e-ink tablet courtesy of a friend who was upgrading. I use that thing constantly. That said, I still have to write things out by hand to connect with them.

When it comes to software, the options are virtually endless. There's note-taking software like OneNote, Notion, or Joplin (an open-source alternative to OneNote).

Many of these options allow you to do e-ink notes as well if you have a tablet or system that supports that kind of input.

In addition to that, many of the various types of writing software have systems for organizing your notes and research in them. Scrivener, QuollWriter (an open-source alternative to Scrivener), and Plottr all have excellent options for notetaking. Then there are services like World Anvil, which give you the ability to do a rather impressive amount of work in them. The only downside with that, however, is if you want it private, you have to pay.

If all of that sounds like just too damn much, then you could go the route of a typed document on your computer. If you use headers, most word processing software has a "navigation" function that will let you categorize and group things under headers and sub headers, which will enable rapid navigation between topics. This is also a function available to you in Google Docs.

I cannot give you a single organization system that will solve all your woes, unfortunately. But all the tools I mentioned are out there, and many of them are open-source or inexpensive if programs like Scrivener and Plottr are too much, or if the Microsoft suite is not your speed.

I'll be talking a little more about writing programs in the chapter on drafting, but some do have excellent organization tools I felt were worth mentioning.

When to Stop Researching

All right, we've gone through all of this chapter on research, and now we have to hit a point where we talk about when to stop. When enough is enough.

As I've said right along, you do not need to be an expert on everything to use it in your book or be an author (unless you're writing a book where you claim to be an expert in your subject matter—then you absolutely must be one). You don't need to research every single thing to death, and accuracy, while always appreciated, is not always make or break in fiction. So long as you research at least those five things I mentioned at the start of the chapter, you can get away with a lot.

Non-fiction is a different creature, though, and I acknowledge that. Depending on the type of book you're writing, you may or may not need to do a great deal of research along with it. While writing this book and its companion, I didn't need to do much outside research since the majority of what I am sharing with you comes from personal experience. I did, however, fact check myself about things like programs and so on to ensure I was sharing accurate information.

The adage of "write what you know" is also applicable here. If you write about subjects you're familiar with, you can cut down on research dramatically. If you do want to include things you don't know, though, research may prove to be a must even if it's cursory.

The point at which you stop researching is when you have enough that you can write a story that doesn't break immersion. For example, if you're writing a fantasy story, you don't need to become an expert on xenobiology. Your dragons can breathe fire without you explaining how. Magic can break the laws of physics so long as it doesn't break its own rules. Medieval-flavored high fantasy doesn't need to conform perfectly to a specific year in history to be enjoyable.

If you're writing combat, maybe all you need to do is watch a few YouTube videos about the type of combat you're writing about and see what you can do to look into what it might be like to experience the kind of thing you're talking about. Spending ten minutes looking something up on an internet search may be more than enough for you to put a detail into your story that deepens a scene.

There is a relatively common thing I run into, too: authors who research forever rather than writing because research feels safer. I'm not here to shame anybody, but if all you do is research and never write, you're clearly dealing with a struggle that is less about data collection and more about anxiety around writing the story.

To address non-fiction, the point at which you stop researching is when you have sufficient data for your book. For some books, this might be a much heavier lift than others. If you are writing a true-crime book, then there's a high chance you are going to be deep into the research sphere, interviewing people where possible, studying articles, and looking at all the information available to you. Where you stop is directly related to whether or not you've sufficiently uncovered the story. With a work like this one, I stopped researching as soon as I verified the accuracy of whatever it was I was saying at the time. With a memoir, you might double-check dates, names, and events, but you aren't going to need to re-learn everything there is to know about something you lived through.

This whole chapter on research is about giving you tools you can use rather than telling you exactly how much you should research or trying to scare you off from writing if you don't spend ten years learning all the "correct" information. When in doubt, just do your best and have beta readers check things out for you, or have an editor fact check. That's one of the things we do.

You'd be amazed what percentage of my job is double-checking facts like when was cross stitch invented and how long would it take to bleed out from a gut wound. Not everyone has the benefit of having an editor to help them out with this kind of thing because, frankly, editing is expensive. However, the fact is that we do exist, and we can help supplement your research by doing some of our own.

Beta readers, too, may well have knowledge. My beta readers are folks who know things about a lot of the content I write on. I've also asked people with specific knowledge to read my books before because I wanted to ensure accuracy. So even if you're not an expert personally, you might well be able to fake it if someone else is willing to double-check. You don't need to write in a vacuum.

As such, research is all about creating a sense of immersion and realism. Does it need to be entirely accurate and perfect to feel real? No. Of course not. I write about angels, demons, orcs, elves, magic, and CIA agents. I write in Boston using locations I am familiar with and subjects I know because, by using those things as a backdrop, I can make the fantastical stuff feel more real. That's the whole goal. Make the story feel real, and allow the reader to suspend disbelief.

If you know enough to accomplish that? You're good.

Summary

Throughout this chapter, we have talked deeply about research for your book. How to do it, where to go, and what you really need to know about hunting down answers. We discussed some sources you can utilize for research and how to put all that research together in a way that works for you.

Key Takeaways

- Research is not optional for several key points and should be deployed liberally when addressing:
    - Cultures that are not your own
    - Technology in your work's time period
    - Injuries and damage
    - How to represent mental illness
    - Weaponry and combat
- You can use many sources to research your book! These sources must be properly vetted, but there are many options for exploring information for your work.
- Organizing your research can take many forms, including printed resources, using a program to organize your notes, and more. Whatever method you take, you should be able to look through your research quickly to find what you need.
- There are times when research in and of itself becomes an obstacle authors use to prevent themselves from having to work further. Knowing when to stop researching and get to writing is an important skill!

Chapter Four
The Drafting Process

This chapter is not about craft. It's about techniques and troubleshooting. There are many books on craft out there, and I may one day add to that number, but for now, I want to focus on techniques to get you out of tight spots and focus on how to get your project *done* rather than the details of refining your prose.

With that in mind, there will be a list of resources available on my website (http://www.ehprybylski.com) where you can find the books and sources I have personally found useful in my career as an author and editor.

Writing Programs

There are many, many writing programs out in the world, and almost every writer will have their preferences to their method of digitizing their text. Some of these programs have more bells and whistles than others; some are expensive; some are open-source and freely available. Choosing a writing software that works best for you is a journey of personal exploration. I know someone who uses GitHub to write in. I don't know how, but they do. I respect their dedication to it.

I'm sure there are programs I don't mention out there that could prove useful to authors when it comes to drafting their novel, and I'm sure more will be developed after this book is published. However, this list presents the ones I am aware of currently. All the paid programs on this list come with trial periods, so you can dabble with ones you find interesting and see what fits your workflow best. There's no wrong answer here!

Microsoft Word

An oldie but a goodie, Microsoft Word is responsible for a solid 65% of the market share when it comes to word processing. It is the keystone for office life and has many, many features that make it an ideal place to handle certain aspects of writing, like headings, using macros, and other such things.

Word provides a blank canvas and has no information management system, however, so if you take notes or need to reference materials, you will need to do so outside the software. Also, moving chapters and scenes around can be difficult if you aren't using headings to identify them.

Google Docs

This one is becoming increasingly popular, much to my dismay. While it is a perfectly reasonable place to write short documents or shared writing projects—and it's free—Google Docs doesn't provide a particularly good interface. It also will begin to lag and hang when working on documents longer than a few pages.

It can be useful to share things with colleagues, friends, and co-writing partners, but be aware that you're going to want to have a separate file for every few chapters, or every chapter, to ensure there's no lag. Downloading all those into a single document for editing and formatting at a later date *will* prove annoying. There are many known issues with Google Docs downloads, though, and I know more than one editor who has spent hours tearing out their hair trying to handle weird formatting problems that come from that exercise.

What Google Docs *does* have going for it is that it is cloud-based, so there is far less fear of losing your work in the event of an unexpected computer disaster. However, you can get around that with other writing software by either uploading the document to a cloud or backing it up on physical mediums like USB drives.

Open Office, Libre Office, and other open-source products

If you don't have reliable internet, find Google Docs stifling and limiting, or you either don't have the money to purchase Microsoft Word or don't want to pay for it, the open-source office programs provide a viable alternative.

They don't have the same power or design elements of Microsoft Word, and I have noticed they often start having issues with tracked changes and comments if they are switching between Word and the open-source software. They do, however, work just fine in a pinch and will allow you to write your draft and provide formatting tools for things like headings.

Headings and so on are more important than you think, but those usually come in the formatting phase of manuscript writing, so it's not entirely necessary to drafting.

Scrivener

This is getting into the realm of author-specific software and leaving the generic word processors. Many authors swear by Scrivener for its ability to keep notes, plotlines, and characters all within the same program's ecosystem. You can also export your Scrivener file into an ebook format if you choose to. I don't have any personal affection for the program myself, and have found other programs do the same work for a smaller price tag of $0.00, but taste is taste, and Scrivener is undeniably a giant in the market.

That said, I have noticed formatting issues when documents are exported from Scrivener into Microsoft Word. One of the biggest things I've come across is it deleting all curly quotes or inconsistently using curly quotes and straight quotes. There are other oddities on occasion with the formatting too, so use care.

Also, as an edge over its open-source competition, it does allow you to apply text styles.

yWriter and QuollWriter

Much as Open Office and Libre Office are to Word, yWriter and QuollWriter are to Scrivener. They are open-source alternatives to Scrivener, and I like them both almost equally. QuollWriter has some interesting and fun warm-up tools as well as access to a beta reading community within the program natively. yWriter offers a nice text-to-voice option to allow you to listen to your book as part of the editing process. QuollWriter's interface is sleeker and prettier than yWriter's, but overall, I personally find yWriter my preferred program. I do all my drafting in it unless I am writing a short story.

However, as far as formatting goes, these programs have a bit of a weakness as they don't use headings or have a great deal of text formatting options beyond bold, underline, and italic. Personally, I do my drafting in yWriter and then apply headings and edit in Word. I don't mind that extra step since I do my editing in Word anyway (more on that in the editing chapter).

Plottr

While one does not draft in Plottr (nor do they simply walk into Mordor), I would be seriously remiss if I didn't mention it. This piece of software has quickly become one of my most valuable tools when planning and writing a novel. It is home to my series bible. What that is, if you don't know, is information about locations, characters, factions, plot plans, etc. I need to keep my series consistent. Plottr also helps me with my book planning. I cannot speak highly enough of this software.

It provides you with a large number of templates to help you structure your novel and an excellent hub for all your series' information. I purchased it during NaNoWriMo 2022, and I already cannot imagine my life without it. If you have a complex series with multiple timelines to manage (or multiple series, since you can have multiple book series in it with ease), you will find this software provides you with an irreplaceable resource in putting it all together.

World Anvil

World Anvil was originally created to be more of a product for TTRPG (tabletop role-playing game) enthusiasts to use to build their worlds. However, it has application for speculative fiction authors to help build their world as well as hold their writing. It has a free version where you can do a lot of world building and have access to many incredible tools. However, in order to keep your world private, you need to pay for it.

My main caution with World Anvil is that it will inherently lead you to over-developing your world because of the many possible layers you can add. You can micromanage cities, economies, characters, countries, and so much more. The wiki-like nature of it leads to easy navigation, and the fact that it does have a writer/author end of the pool means there are tools I never explored as a GM (Game Master). I just advise caution if you tend to be struck with world-builder's disease because you will never hit the end of it.

Sustainable Writing Habits

Please note that I am starting this segment at midnight after writing 10,000 words on the launch day of my second novel. So, all this advice can be squinted at with suspicion because clearly, I am a paragon of my own advice.

Joking aside, sustainable writing habits are an important facet of long-term career success. If you want to write more than one book and have a career as an author, writing a book has to be a *repeatable* experience for you.

More than that, it has to be repeatable in a way that you can do regularly over a long period of time. In order to do that, you need to cultivate good habits. Not like me.

Shh. Don't look at me like that. You can pry my caffeine-fueled hyperfocus sessions from my cold, dead (probably cramping) hands.

The key to sustainability for us as authors is learning what our goals are and making measurable steps toward them. How many words you write in a day might not be important to you. Maybe it's five. Maybe it's fifty. Maybe you write every day, or maybe you write once a week. Whatever your life allows you to do is what you are after.

These targets, goals, and abilities will fluctuate with time and life events, too. If you're going through a time of hardship, have demands of your time you cannot ignore (like children or partners), or maybe have a really demanding period at work, *don't be unkind to yourself* if you fall a little behind. We are, after all, human. And creative work is *hard*.

With all of that said, there are a few principles you can use to create consistent writing habits. I'm not going to give you exact word counts you should shoot for, but I will include a few averages to give you some ideas of what others do. *There is no obligation to hit those averages*, nor are you any less of a "real writer" for needing to adjust any of these things. The only qualification for being a "real writer" is work toward completing your goals. That's it. That's the whole metric.

Sometimes, being a "real writer" also means taking breaks, handling real life, and knowing that there are things in life you should be there for. Don't miss important moments because you're head down in a manuscript any more than you should miss them for any other job. Those important moments are why we are here, after all.

All the various principles I talk about below will invite creativity into your world. There are, of course, about a million more things we could discuss here, including flow states, certain apps and programs that help with that, and how meditation can affect the mind and help us create space for creativity, which I will get into in the next segment. However, I don't want to get too granular into prescribing specific practices for you. What I wanted to do is provide broad strokes ideas for you to explore and make your own.

All these points are mere suggestions. What works for you is going to be what works *for you*. You can create a sustainable writing practice that looks like nothing anyone else has used before if that's what suits your life. As I keep hammering into in this book, the only "wrong" way to go about this is to create a writing practice that doesn't work for you long term.

Also, I want to caution against trying to wring productivity out of yourself as if you were a sponge. While there will be times and moments that it feels like you're dragging ideas out of yourself kicking and screaming, your creativity should feel more like a spring pouring out of an underground aquifer than it should like water being wrung from a dishrag. If it feels like the latter, something isn't working.

In many cases, that "something" might be that your life has other needs right now (children, partners, work, etc.), and that's all right. There is a season for all things, and there will be times in our lives when our creativity just isn't very high. I've been wrestling with one of those myself. My husband broke his foot and has needed a great deal of care, and that has resulted in a large amount of fatigue on my end. I just haven't had the mental energy to write, and as a result, I have missed several deadlines and disappointed people. That sometimes happens.

Be kind to yourself and make sure that whatever productivity strategies you use leave room for the realities of life. As I said earlier, we are not machines. We are human beings with needs, wants, goals, and experiences. Don't hurt yourself to create your art. That kind of self-harm does not create a sustainable writing career. If it does, it will come at the cost of your mental and physical health and relationships with people around you. Don't be that person. (I'm just going to stare in Earnest Hemingway's direction.)

When writing seriously, set a reasonable and achievable goal for your writing sessions

Note that I said, "when writing seriously." I am not constantly writing. Sometimes, I am editing; other times, I am marketing; and other times, I am taking a break. However, when I am zeroed in on a manuscript and trying to get it *done*, I regularly will set goals for word count. They're not inflexible, but they're things to shoot for. The writing software I use (yWriter) allows me to set up goals for time and/or word count, and I feel like that is a good balance.

For some people, they are going to sit in the chair until they have written x number of words. For others, they will write for a certain amount of time a day, and what they get is what they get. Both of those things are equally valid. I tend to write during intense writing sessions where I zero in on my work with laser focus for many hours at a time. This sometimes lasts for a few weeks, and then I collapse into a smoldering ball at the end and spend a few weeks needing to decompress. Everyone has their own writing patterns, and while mine might not be sustainable for some people, it seems to work for me.

To give you some more specific numbers, an average professional writer often shoots for around 1,000 words in a day. Depending on font size and spacing, that equates to around two pages in Microsoft Word with default settings (size 12 Times New Roman, single spaced, 8.5x11 pages). Remember, however, that number is based on others' experiences.

You might find you cannot write that many words in a day consistently, and if you can't? Okay. Set your goal to what you feel is achievable for you. That goal can shift a little and slide as necessary. It may take a while for you to find your pace, so try a few different goals and see what feels best and what you can do most regularly. If it's 50 words, 100 words, 500 words, or any other number, that's just fine.

If you're shooting for time spent, I'd say if you can work on your writing for half an hour a day, you will be able to make good progress. An hour a day is ideal, but I also recognize that many of us just do not have that kind of time. And if all you can manage is about fifteen minutes? That's fine. Whatever number works for you is what works for you.

Do not measure yourself by someone else's yardstick

The quickest way to burn yourself out is to set goals based on what everyone else is doing that do not work for you and your life. I have met people who attempted to shame or guilt or deride others into writing at what they considered "the true pace of a professional," and that just doesn't work. All it does is give people anxiety, cause misery, and make people feel like they should quit. That sort of attitude damages the industry as a whole and silences many voices who have valuable things to share and stories the world may need, or at the very least enjoy.

To show the contrast in what is out there, I have a friend who bangs out a novel every week or two, and I am in awe of what she can accomplish so consistently. For me, I publish about once a year and write one to two books in that time. We are both equally professional, and we are both equally valid—we just operate differently.

There is absolutely no "official" measure about how you "should" write. The only "true way" is to find your pace, your measures, and what you can achieve on a regular basis. Nothing else. Heck, I know people who take 5-7 years to write a novel. We cannot all be Brandon Sanderson, and there's absolutely nothing wrong with that. You don't need to be Brandon Sanderson. You just need to be you.

Sustainable means repeatable over a long period of time

Right now, there is a rapid release publishing boom happening. Some authors put out a book a month or even more frequently. However, that boom is also causing a lot of busts. What I mean by that is many authors see that, think they want to try it, and end up burning out hard and fast and disappointing themselves and their fans because that pace is *not* sustainable long term. The secret to rapid release is to do what I am doing with this book and its second volume: writing them both in advance, editing them both in advance, and then releasing them close together.

Most of these rapid release success stories have a large bank of books they've been building up over time and preparing and then doing a massive push to launch them all one after another. It's not a bad marketing plan and raises awareness of their work quickly, but it also comes with other people thinking that these successful authors write and edit and typeset and prepare for that many launches that quickly when, in reality, it's often an illusion.

I say "often" because I know people for whom it isn't an illusion, but those friends often burn out hard and fast and then either have to leave the industry entirely or take a long vacation and return in a more sustainable model for their future releases.

Publishing is not a sprint, it is a marathon. If you want to make writing a career choice for yourself, you need to look at the long term. What can you do over time? If you pour on all the steam right out of the gate in a 5k marathon, you're not going to reach the finish line. Instead, you're going to end up panting, wheezing, and exhausted in the first hundred meters. Writing is very similar. We should look at our long-term goals and assess what we need to get there.

Rapid release can be a highly effective strategy for publication. I'm not going to pretend it isn't, but it's best employed when you have written the books in advance, prepared them in advance, and then release them close together so you don't create an immense strain on yourself. That strain burns writers out because creatives aren't usually meant to put out incredibly high volume all the time.

We are not machines. We are human beings who need to recharge, enjoy life, and manage our mental health, no matter what certain elements of business seem to believe these days.

Create a writing ritual and/or a writing space

The space I'm talking about can be a mental space just as much as a physical one. For example, my writing ritual is to have a cup of tea on hand, pull up some instrumental music to listen to in the background, and open my writing software. From there, I frequently use the Sukha app to time my writing and carve it into pieces.

My husband, on the other hand, really likes to go to a local coffee shop with me where we sit once or twice a week for an hour or so and write together with our laptops back-to-back. We also usually get bagel sandwiches.

Setting aside time for your writing and creating room for your mind to unfold a little and stretch is key to maximizing your productivity and entering a flow state, so however you want to do that is what works for you. Whether it is writing at the same time every day, having a certain playlist you listen to, creating an order of operations to what you open when, sitting in a specific spot in your house... There are a nearly infinite number of ways you can create space for your writing in your life and mind. As with the rest of these things, the key for you is going to be to try things and find what works for you.

Whatever ritual or space you create, however, you should make sure it's something you actively enjoy. It should, as Marie Kondo puts it, "spark joy." If it doesn't, you will feel less creative and end up fighting against lack of enjoyment in order to achieve your goals.

I strongly suggest finding a way to add pleasure to it. Whether it's a mug of tea, a glass of wine, a cup of coffee, some chocolate, or your favorite music, find the things that make you feel safe, contented, and at ease. Once those needs are met, and once that head space is achieved, you will discover creativity will happen. If you are having trouble with creativity—the dreaded "writers' block"—I address that later on in this chapter. Don't despair.

Make time to daydream

This may seem foolish, but in today's world, we are pressured to constantly go, go, go! If we aren't producing something, somehow, we are falling behind. That mentality just doesn't work for creativity. In this productivity practice of yours, you need to build in some time for daydreaming. This may look like taking an extra five minutes in the shower. Or it could mean having your coffee without staring at your email first thing in the morning.

It doesn't need to be a very long time to be effective, but build some time into your day to let your mind wander a bit. That wander time will lead to idea generation and creativity. Plus, it will cut down on the mental "static" we so often hear when we pack our schedules to the gills.

Why Comparison Kills Creativity

I mentioned this briefly in the last segment about not measuring yourself to someone else's stick, but this is something I really want to emphasize, so it gets its own whole segment. "Comparison kills creativity" is one of those things I think all creatives need to tattoo on the inside of their eyelids.

While writing, you need to understand that you cannot, and should not, compare yourself to anybody else. Worry about comps (comparable works) when you're done and trying to either get representation or prepare for marketing. And even then, you're just looking for things that are in the same ballpark as your work.

The thing that destroys new writers the fastest is going to be saying, "I'm not as good as 'x'." Part of the problem with that is it's like trying to compare Beethoven to Lady Gaga. Whatever you think about either composer, they are both incredibly skilled and have captured the minds and hearts of their respective time periods. However, if you put them next to each other, it can be difficult to compare them through anything but the lens of personal taste. I happen to very much like both for different reasons. I also wouldn't compare Jethro Tull to VNV Nation. Similar problems.

You do not need to be "as good as" anyone. You need to learn to write your stories well. That is your whole job. Write what you want to write and do so with aplomb. Just because you don't write in the same voice as Neil Gaiman or Stephen King does not make you not worth publishing. Sure, both of them are highly polished masters of the craft, but if you put the two of them next to each other, you would be hard pressed to make a comparison unless you're already an expert yourself.

While you are writing, particularly early in your career, you need to set aside the idea that your first draft needs to be anything but finished. If you chronically feel like you aren't any good and that nobody will care and no one will buy your book, you will psych yourself out of accomplishing anything. Then you will stall out and end up frustrated, depressed, and disappointed.

First drafts don't need to be good; they only need to be finished. While some authors write one draft, edit while writing, and publish it (and I have feelings on that, but I'm not going to get into them here), that isn't how the vast majority of authors write, and it's not how I'd advise anyone new to the craft. There are outliers, and there will always be outliers, but if you are putting pressure on yourself to create perfection on the first try, you will never get off the ground.

If you are early in your writing career—and if you have bought this book, I assume you likely are—you should view your craft the same way a beginning musician views learning their first few songs. As I have mentioned elsewhere, I am a musician. A violinist, in fact. I have taught beginning violin on and off for many years. Every violinist, no matter how good they become, starts off sounding like a sack of cats going down a staircase. Screeching, thunking, dismay, and disaster. (Please do not put cats in a sack to demonstrate the sound to anybody or test the theory. It would not be kind to the cats, the staircase, or you when they get loose.)

If we view our writing as the same kind of progression of art, your first drafts are you learning the piece, learning techniques, and exploring the various portions of the song and the instrument. It takes time. While your mileage may vary, most of the time, it takes about a year of consistent practice to get from the sack of cats down a staircase sound to something halfway decent.

Comparing a beginning violinist to Itzhak Perlman, one of the world's most famous and skilled violinists, would be cruel and unfair. So why do that to yourself with your writing? I'm not certain why, but writing seems to fall into this liminal space where people don't understand that it requires just as much thought, dedication, effort, time, and study to get good at as any other art.

Keep in mind that while you are drafting, you are just starting your journey with that book. Expecting or demanding perfection of yourself while you are doing so is not kind and is one of the fastest ways to ruin for new writers I have ever seen. Give yourself room to breathe and just write. Editing comes later. Comparisons come later. For now? Just put words on the page and let go of the notion of writing something perfect. Shoot for something good. And if you can't shoot for something good? Shoot for something finished.

Flow States and Focus Techniques

The concept of "flow states" is one more often used in coding, business, or sports. It's an idea I started exploring when I met my friend Stephen Puri, owner of the Sukha Company. While I am not going to attempt to explain everything about the neuroscience that he does, if you ever get a chance to talk to him, I do want to address the idea.

A "flow state" is a place where nothing else is in your head but what you're working on. It's that feeling of everything just kind of gliding along smoothly. When the words just *happen*. I have been in one of those through most of writing this book, to be honest. Unlike a lot of my fiction where I wrestle to get words on the page, this book has more or less just fallen out of my fingers all at once.

That experience is one we strive for when creating our writing routines, and in order to achieve it, you're going to need to do a few things to get your brain into that space. I'm going to go over them in brief here, but the science of flow states is fascinating, and I heavily advise you to at least look up a few YouTube videos on the subject to learn more about how to utilize them for your purposes.

While flow states are *not necessary* for the craft of writing or for you to be successful, you may find that learning about how to access them and how to use them will result in a far higher productivity state than you might otherwise achieve. They are worth understanding and attempting to learn how to tap into for that reason alone.

The forthcoming guidance is geared toward helping you understand a method of getting the most out of your writing time in an ideal setting and how to create space for that to happen. If you can't use these things right now? That's fine. You have data for when you can, and data never hurt anybody. Well, Data did, but *Star Trek* doesn't count, okay?

As I said at the start, you do not absolutely need to utilize flow states in order to write. You might be able to get a few words here and there without them, and some folks' lives are just plain not structured to allow for such things at this time. There is nothing wrong or shameful with that, and you are not barred from writing if you can't hit a flow state. Whatever you need to do for yourself is what you need to do for yourself, and we as humans just cannot make our brains "do the thing" sometimes.

Cut out all distraction if at all possible

In order to enter a flow state, you absolutely must be in a space and time when there are no distractions. The reason for this is, every time you end up breaking out of what you're doing, you interrupt the flow state. There are neurochemical reasons why this is a thing, but since I lack a strong understanding of neuroscience, I'm just going to say: Distraction makes the brain juice stop flowing as well.

When you prepare to write for whatever time you have, do your best to shut down distractions. Put your phone on silent or Do Not Disturb. Close out of messaging applications. Do your best to ensure people around you know not to disturb you for a set amount of time (if possible—children are going to do what they do, and if they need care, there's no avoiding that). You also might want to invest in some noise cancelling headphones. Whether you listen to music as you write or not, the noise cancellation can do a lot to close out things that will drag you out of flow.

A note about music here: The threshold for tolerating working to music or ambient sound is going to be different for each person. I cannot handle music with lyrics, for example, because my instinct is to sing along with them, and then I end up inserting those lyrics into whatever I'm writing. Obviously, that is less than ideal. However, I do love some dark academia playlists with ambient rain, thunder, and fireplace sounds. I also enjoy the coffee house ambience videos that have quiet but inaudible voices, silverware, and jazz.

Experiment with some different types of music and sound to create different atmospheres. I also particularly like the "Sword Coast Soundscapes" pieces on YouTube because they can help me set a scene and feel of a piece. Since I write urban fantasy, having fantasy noises in the background can very much help me get into my piece. You can also find that certain works require different music. If I'm writing a heavily emotional piece and listening to something happy and bouncy in the background, it will throw me off. I tend to pair my music to the scenes I'm working on sort of like a sommelier pairs their wine with your dinner. Your mileage may vary.

Optimize your workspace for flow

If your workspace is scattered, and you have to do a lot of work to gather the things you need in order to continue your efforts, you are not going to enter a state of flow anywhere near as easily. As such, make sure the things you need for your project are in reach. I also suggest having a drink handy, since things like thirst will break you out of flow, too.

When I'm really digging in deep to writing, I make sure I have some water, all my apps are closed, my phone is on its charger and out of my way or out of sight entirely, and I have a comfortable chair, good keyboard, and good mouse. If you are writing in a space that is not physically comfortable for you to work in for whatever period of time you intend on working for, you will struggle to enter a flow state. Remember, the goal here is to eliminate distraction, and discomfort is a distraction.

Also, if your workspace is a mess, it *will* distract you. I say this as someone whose desk perpetually looks like a tornado went through it, so understand that there's no judgment happening at all. Right now, I have several medications, catnip spray, a container of parmesan from last night's takeout, my sketch pencils, some tennis balls, a back scratcher, and some sewing needles on my desk. Those are just the things right in front of me. I'm not going to torture you with a full inventory, but please don't think I'm judging you because frankly, I'm guilty of this one.

Science and psychology, however, show that visual clutter and distraction do pull people out of flow. If you can minimize your visual input and work in a tidy space, it will help you stick to your flow state without getting distracted by thoughts of, "Oh yeah, I should put that away."

Most writing programs have the option of a full screen mode that hides everything on your screen except a box with the words you're writing in it. They even hide the formatting tools. Even Microsoft Word has this function. Usually, it's called some variety of "focus mode" or "full screen" mode. Using that helps minimize distraction in the form of notifications in your task bar.

If you need something further, you can try an app like Sukha to keep you focused. I have a group on there for writers, and it's an excellent way to both work together and keep yourself separate. Centered has built-in timers, task management, and so on. It's a great program. No, they're not paying me to say that; I just really do like the software.

Get good sleep, hydration, and food

If you are hungry, exhausted, and dehydrated, your brain is not going to enter a flow state. It just won't. The only exception to this is if you have ADHD, autism, or a similar neurotype as you might end up in hyperfocus mode, which is basically like a flow state with extra features. Those extra features being that we don't notice we haven't eaten, slept, bathed, or had water in who knows how long. When you finally emerge from the hyperfocus rabbit hole, you often realize you feel like that wrung-out sponge I mentioned earlier in the chapter. It's not healthy to get into for long periods of time. My solution to this is to set timers to drag me out of hyperfocus headspaces.

For non-neurodivergent folks, however, unlocking that flow state means your physical needs have to be met. Maybe have a light snack before you start working, or have a snack on hand while you write, though make sure it's something you can just pick up and eat like grapes, cheese cubes, or other pre-sliced and pre-prepared things. You should also make sure you have a glass of water or are otherwise adequately hydrated. You can also write with a drink nearby. I do so regularly.

Sleep is the last one. If you are not well-rested, your brain will struggle to be creative. When it comes to the hierarchy of needs, creativity is one of the first things that suffers when we become stressed and when our bodies are under-performing due to a lack of care. If you want creativity to happen, you need to make sure sleep is something you take seriously. You cannot draw water from an empty well.

This is one of the main reasons why folks dealing with life issues struggle with creativity. Our ability to enter flow and find our creative selves vanishes when our survival mode comes online because creativity is considered an expendable thing. From an evolutionary point of view, base survival is vastly more important to the continuation of an organism's life than creativity. While creativity is very important, in times of immediate duress, survival needs take center stage for obvious reasons.

Many of us in modern society are locked into a low-level survival state at almost all times. The constant pressures we face of merely trying to feed ourselves, keep a roof over our heads, and ensure our needs are met are intensive. For many people, that constant struggle leaves them unable to do more than stare at the television for an hour before bed at the end of the day. If that's where you are, there's no judgment. You need to take care of your health and safety first. Just know that, until you find more stability, your creativity will take a hit.

I won't say creativity is *impossible* under those conditions because for many, the act of creating is a kind of catharsis and allows them to slip away from their stress and into a world far removed from their problems. That is absolutely a thing, but in this case, we're talking about the ability to access flow states more than we are specifically talking about creativity itself. And flow requires the body and brain to be in good working order.

Go into your writing session with defined goals

This isn't a need for everyone, but if you go into your flow session with measurable, specific goals, you will find it easier to meet them. The keys here are *specific* and *measurable*. If you just say you want to "write," that's not really measurable except by whether or not there are words on the page at all for an indeterminate amount of time.

One way to create specific and defined goals is to use a timer. I mentioned the Sukha app before, and there's a timer function in it that allows you to set up Pomodoro segments and take breaks before coming back into your flow state. It also yells at you if you open websites like YouTube and Facebook and other distractions, which I like.

The "Pomodoro Method" is, essentially, breaking your time up into 25-minute chunks with 5-minute breaks in between. So you focus intensely for that 25 minutes and then stand up, stretch, get water, go to the bathroom, or whatever you want to between them. While the 25/5 method is the tradition, you can set whatever length of time you feel most effective for you.

As someone who gets sucked into flow states for unhealthy periods of time, however, I do suggest you limit yourself to no more than an hour without a stretch, water, and change your focus break. It's important for your eyes to change focal points to prevent macular degeneration, so make sure you are regularly looking away from your monitors at something far away during your breaks.

Try not to change gears mid-flow

If you stumble across something you need to look up while you're writing, you have a choice. If it's something you really need to know more about in order to move forward, you can break and go do some study. That will, however, mess with your flow. Changing gears necessitates you leaving your current flow state to either start a different one or ditch it altogether.

When this happens as I'm writing, I will typically leave myself placeholder information in brackets. For example, I was working on my current project and didn't remember what those inflatable boats used by SpecOps and other divisions were called (they're Zodiac boats, and it's a brand name). So I just put [inflatable boat] in its place and kept writing. Using those brackets means they're easy to find and replace later, too, since I rarely use those specific pieces of punctuation in my writing. You could choose a different character, but the point is to make it easy to identify so you can later go back. Some popular ones are ~, [, and {. If you use those in your fiction for whatever reason, you could also do something like ## or VVV to replace the word. There are a lot of options to choose from and, as with so many other things in this book, you can play with many ideas and see what you like best.

When you are actively in flow, breaking it to go do something else destroys the work you put in getting into your flow state to begin with. Multitasking renders it impossible in its entirety, no matter how confident you are that you're a great multitasker. Yes, you. And me. And everyone else with ADHD. I'm talking directly to you. You might be able to do it a lot of the time, but doing it during writing will ruin your ability to enter a flow state and result in chaos and confusion.

How Many Words Should "X" Be?

I suspect this may be the shortest sub-section in the book, but in the spirit of giving people concrete and actionable parameters to plan their writings, here are some numbers you should be aware of as you start work. While the next book in this two-book set is going to be more about the business end of publishing, word count is one of those things you need to know early.

These numbers are averages, and very few of them are hard limits or definitions, but you should shoot for ballpark ranges in order to conform with genre expectations or, for example, identifying the type of work you are creating.

Different Types of Pieces

- Flash Fiction: 1,000 words or less
- Short Story: 1,000 - 30,000 words
- Novella: 30,000 - 50,000 words
- Novels: 50,000 words and up

Word Count Averages by Audience Age (2022)

- Adult Fiction: 50,000 words and up
- Young Adult: 45,000 - 80,000 words
- Middle Grade: 20,000 - 60,000 words
- Children's Chapter Books: 5,000 - 20,000 words
- Picture Books: 250 - 1,000 words

Word Count Averages by Genre (2022)

- Speculative Fiction: 70,000 - 120,000 words
- Historical Fiction: 80,000 - 100,000 words
- Horror: 80,000 - 100,000 words
- Action/Adventure: 80,000 - 95,000 words
- Contemporary Fiction: 70,000 - 90,000 words
- Romance: 70,000 - 90,000 words
- Erotica: 40,000 - 60,000 words
- Literary Fiction: 70,000 - 90,000 words

These numbers are averages based roughly on the numbers of book lengths I have been able to dig up. They all fall into about the average expected range with historical fiction, epic fantasy, and epic sci-fi tending to run long. These word counts *are* a little spongy in places, but generally speaking, you really want to shoot for the middle of the pack. Neither too long nor too short; you want your book to be "just right."

Word counts, when it comes to books, determine a few things. First and foremost, the word count has a direct

The Drafting Process

correlation to editing costs. Many editors charge by the word, though some also charge by the hour, depending on their personal tastes.

Secondly, your word count determines your page count when printing. The industry average is about 250 words per page. This number may go up or down a little depending on format, font choices, and formatting decisions, but on average, you are expecting around that. A larger book is, by its nature, more expensive to print and thus more expensive to ship because fewer fit in a box. That's simple math and physics at work.

Many people think that the answer to this conundrum is to cut corners and hire a cheaper editor, or eschew editing altogether in favor of using something like Grammarly. I'm not here to shame anybody who is struggling financially. However, we must recognize that publication costs are one of those arenas that decide how successful your book is going to be.

Let me just tuck that soapbox under my desk for the next book, though. This one is about getting the writing done, and talking about the cost of doing business and publication is the next volume's problem. It's not something you need to think about too hard while working on your first draft.

For now, just be aware that you're shooting for the sweet spots in the middle of those ranges with some wiggle room on either side depending on your genre, age range, and type of work in question. When it comes to targeting younger audiences, remember that the younger the audience, the shorter the book ought to be.

The last number I'm going to throw your way is about chapter length because I see that question asked frequently. Average chapter length, much like book length, varies depending on age range. For adult novels, you are looking at between 1,700 and 3,000 words on average per chapter. To break that down into printed book pages (250 words/page), we are looking at between about 7 to 12 pages per chapter for a work of fiction. You may find yourself having some chapters either longer or shorter than that range. There's nothing wrong with the occasional outlier as the story requires.

The only real hard and fast guidance I have is that you should try and shoot for *relatively even length* for the majority of your chapters. Some may be longer, some may be shorter, but reasonable consistency will make your book more accessible for readers. If your chapter length is all over the place, it may make the book feel very choppy and hard to negotiate.

Also, when I say "consistent," I mean within a few hundred words of each other. Most of my chapters in fiction are between 1,500 and 1,800 words, for example. I don't shoot for a hard and fast word count because that would be peculiar pacing, but within 300–500 words of one another is a good range.

Combating Writer's Block

Before I can tell you how to combat writers' block, I want to address the fact that whether writer's block exists at all is a rather hotly contested issue in some circles. There are some people who think it's just an excuse for not writing. Others believe it's very real. Myself, I think it's somewhere in between.

Struggling with creativity when in stressful situations is a very real, very common experience. Also, running into times where you just plain don't know what to do next is something everyone experiences at some point in their writing career. What I'm unsure of is the idea that "writer's block" is a specific thing that exists in a vacuum or that it has a singular cure because it can be a multifaceted problem born of a whole collection of elements that require different solutions.

I would liken it to having a fever. A fever in and of itself is a symptom of a different problem, and that problem could be anything from the flu to a life-threatening infection. While you can treat the fever itself through various techniques, you can only do so much if you don't treat the underlying cause. Identifying the cause is absolutely necessary to cure it.

Writer's block is much the same. The inability to write forward on a work is a *symptom* rather than the source of the problem. Diagnosing the cause of the problem will allow us to treat the issue at its core. That, then, will have the end result of the block no longer being a problem.

So, how do we identify the core issue causing writer's block? We have to look at when the block is manifesting because there could be a number of parts at play here. I've mentioned a few of them already in previous sections of the book, but to sum up:

- Physical needs unmet (thirsty, hungry, tired, in pain)
- Physical or psychological issues causing focus problems (medications, health conditions, etc.)
- High stress causing creativity issues
- Distractions causing an inability to access a flow state
- Being unsure where the story is going
- The need to better understand story structure and pacing
- Insufficient planning
- Too much planning
- The story taking an unplanned turn and resulting in a need to readjust the plan
- A feeling that the story (or you) is no good

While I am certain there are other things that cause struggles in getting words down on the page, those are the majority of the specific problems I've seen when talking about having writer's block. As you can see, the underlying issue for some of them is dramatically different than others. If I were to give just blanket advice on treating the symptom (writer's block) rather than the cause, it's like treating the fever but leaving the infection raging.

Many of the things we've talked about in the book so far are options we can use to combat the issues on that list, but sometimes, the only solution is taking a break until outside conditions change. When I can't write because I am dealing with a migraine or a pain flare, no amount of staring at the page and guilting myself will change that. If I miss a dose of my ADHD medication and can't sit still long enough to be able to get words out, obviously, I'm going to run into problems that I can't solve without solving the underlying issue.

When you end up in one of those situations, the best way you can help yourself with your creative block is to sit down and try and figure out the source of it. If the issue you are running into is some form of external factor that isn't the writing itself, you'll need to take care of that problem in order to regain your creative footing.

The problem I have with declaring something writer's block is that it's not inherently solvable. That's not to say the frustration of not being able to write isn't very and completely real, but if we just chalk it up to the ephemeral "writer's block," we rob ourselves of the tools we need to fix the problem. Instead, sit down and spend some time identifying where the difficulty is coming from. That is more likely to get you close to solving your difficulties than anything else.

If you have identified that the problem isn't an external factor, and you're still struggling to write, the thing that usually causes that is a lack of planning or direction. Not knowing the next beat in your story to reach the next important point. Or sometimes, not even knowing what the next important point *is*.

If you find yourself in that situation, it's time to take a step back and reassess. Whether you're a discovery writer or a plotter, knowing what your next plot point is will give you some of the tools you need to move forward, but until you know what it is, you might as well be Abraham wandering around in the desert for forty years.

No matter your methodology for writing your book, when you get to that point where you are just lost, the first place you can look for an answer is going to be the major plot points you have so far. Compare them to what your plan for the ending of the story is and consider what you

The Drafting Process

need to accomplish to get from where you are to where you need to go.

If you haven't planned an ending for the story, then take the time to do so. Even if it's just a rough idea of "and they all lived happily after under the maple tree." If you know what the end of the story is supposed to look like, you can take the steps necessary to achieve that ending.

I understand that planning like that is antithetical to the way some writers prefer to work, and I'm not here to shame anybody for that. However, I have found that discovery writers run into writer's block more frequently than other types of writers do because of their lack of planning.

To be honest, I don't believe that anyone is a pure plotter or a pure discovery writer. I think there's a spectrum in there of people who range from needing more or less structure. That said, I have yet to meet a successful writer who doesn't go into a project with at least a small amount of consideration for where they start, where they end, and maybe a rough concept in their mind of where the story is going to go to get there.

With that in mind, while I don't usually advise doing developmental editing in the middle of the book, if you really cannot get past where you are, you can go backward and review the key events that happen in each chapter to give you an idea of the flow of things. From there, something may jump out at you.

The methodology I use for this is similar to writing an outline, though since it's in retrospect, you can write the name of the chapter and then highlight the important story beats that occur in that chapter before moving on. Doing this will give you a bird's eye view of the story as it sits and may both give you some idea of what the next step is *and* help you assess if it's going in the right direction.

If not, and you've outlined those factors, start thinking about what it is that's stopping you about the story. Do you need to do more world building? Do you need to flesh out some element of the story? Do you need to add a character or kill a character? Are you just bored with the story and not really feeling it? Are you going in a direction that isn't satisfying?

Rather than bashing your head against the wall from the lack of writing, if you analyze things for a while, the missing link may jump out at you. If you need to, put things down for a day or two in order to make sense of them. You can do that.

You aren't less of a writer for taking breaks. Even professionals get stuck. I'm writing this in 2024, and the last book in the *A Song of Ice and Fire* series by George R. R. Martin was written in 2011. His fans are still waiting. Not to take a dig at Martin. His writing isn't to my taste, but my point is that taking a little time to chew over a problem in your novel doesn't in any way make you less of a writer. If Martin is still a writer after twelve years of making his fans wait, I think you're probably okay.

Finally, if you find yourself well and truly stuck on a project with no way forward, there's always the option of setting it aside entirely for a while and working on something else. I've had projects get stuck in my craw more than once and had to change gears to a different book altogether (and sometimes finish that one and write two more in the series) before I was ready to go back to the first one. There's no shame in that.

Not every idea pans out. Not every plan is executable. Sometimes, we hit walls. I've also stripped books down and rewritten them start to finish more than once in order to work out problems I ran into when writing them. If the idea is something extremely important to you that you don't want to give up on entirely, it's all right to put it on the shelf for a while and come back to it later when lightning strikes.

The Act Two Slump

Ah, yes, the dreaded "middle" of the book. The place most authors hit brick walls and start questioning their life choices. Part of the problem with writing the "middle" of the book is that act two (of the three-act structure) *is literally half the book*. It is 50% of your word count, which means you're going to be in it for a very long time.

The beginning is exciting because everything is fresh, shiny, and new (cue Bilbo Baggins, "I'm going on an adventure!"). The ending is exciting because we're wrapping it all up in a shiny bow, and the big climactic battle usually happens there. Or the moment the main characters decide to stay together forever. Or whatever the crux of your story is.

Then you have the middle. It feels like a gelatinous mass of half-baked plot ideas, worries about your own sanity, and characters not doing what you expected them to do. This, naturally, leads to a lot of angst on the part of writers who are trying to make sense of this thing.

So, how do we handle the middle? The same way we handled the rest of it: one step at a time.

The key to the middle of your book is in the planning. Whether you plan it in your head, write notecards and stick them on the wall, or just have a few vague ideas for scenes you want to string together, you have to come up with *something* to get your character from the shiny new beginning to the shiny new ending.

There is a lot of advice out there on how to handle the middle. Everything from "skip around and write scenes that excite you" to "just put your head down and write the damn thing." There's no one singular method that will work for everyone, which you may have noticed is a theme in this book. Much like with writer's block, you can't just brute force a single solution to fix everything that's a challenge, no matter how much we wish we could.

I know for discovery writers, this might make your hair curl a little, but planning is the main way you can break through the wall. Even if it's only planning your next step and not trying to plot out the whole story. I'm not saying you need to be a plotter to be successful, but you do need to at least have a collection of ideas you can pull from. Even if you gather them in a word cloud or jotted down on a sticky note at 3 a.m. after awakening from a dream about ducks at a rave. (Untz *quack,* untz *quack,* untz *quack.*)

In absence of all else, you need to keep your eyes on the prize and consider what the next step that needs to happen is to get you through to the ending.

If you just can't seem to wrestle that bear, then you might need to study story structure. Whether you're a plotter or a discovery writer, a solid understanding of what makes a story *work* will help you when nothing else will because you will have a deeper understanding of the things that go into it.

I'm all about the analogies, I know, but think of it in terms of cooking. If you don't know much about cooking, and you discover halfway through a recipe that you're out of an ingredient, you won't know how to substitute it or if you can get around it. However, if you study cooking enough to know how to get around the lack of an ingredient, you can keep making the dish.

Novel writing is the same in that sense. If you run into a snag but don't understand story structure well, you will end up in trouble. If you find yourself hitting that wall repeatedly, it might be worth taking some time off from your writing to read a book on that subject. I strongly suggest *The Anatomy of Story* by John Truby as well as *Save the Cat* by Blake Snyder. While John Truby is deeply not a fan of Blake Snyder's formula, if you read both, you will have two very different angles on the same problem and may come up with a method that works for you.

Summary

In this chapter, we covered the process of writing your first draft(s). This includes everything from choosing a writing software to work in, to habits that will allow us to keep our career moving forward, to discussions of flow state, and writer's block. It is one of the meatiest chapters in this book and covers many different aspects of the writing process.

Key Takeaways

- Choosing a writing program is more than just jumping onto a bandwagon. They all come with benefits and drawbacks, and it's time well spent to explore the way you operate in different programs and find the combination that works best for you.
- Creating sustainable writing habits is a necessity in our world. If we want to have a long-term writing career, we must be mindful of our needs and take them into account.
- Don't compare yourself to others. It will ruin your creativity and cause you a lot of emotional pain. Instead, take inspiration from others but recognize that your journey is your journey, not theirs.
- There are many techniques to help you cut out distractions during your writing time, and creating a collection of methods that work for you is going to help you get more words down faster and with less frustration.
- Writer's block is a broad collection of things and can be caused by a great many factors. Rather than throwing your hands up, investigate why you're really stuck and address the underlying issue before moving forward.
- Act Two is a challenging behemoth and is the place most authors falter if they are going to stumble. Prepare for this by knowing where you're going and relying on the tension and conflict concepts from the previous chapter.

Chapter Five
Self-Editing

This chapter is designed to help authors edit their own works as best they can. The advice contained herein is *not* intended to replace hiring an editor. While I'm not going to get very deep into the publishing territory in this book, editing is one of those things you shouldn't skimp on. It's one of the costs of doing business.

If you just can't afford to hire an editor, there are ways you can get a manuscript pretty clean without one, but please, don't take the advice in this chapter to suggest you can avoid doing that part of the process. Even I have an editor, and I've been editing professionally for over sixteen years. (Mel's the best. Hi, Mel!)

I am certain there are other tools out there that I am missing from this list, but I am sharing the ones with which I am familiar here. If you find any others, feel free to explore them. But, as I said, be mindful that none of these tools—helpful though they are—can replace the skill and acumen of a human editor, so I don't advise using them in lieu of one when you get to that point in the process.

The Importance of Emotional Distance

Before we start work on editing proper, we have to address an elephant in the room: Our books are our babies. We are extremely close to them, and we have deep and powerful feelings about our work. All authors do. Just like artists feel that way about their various mediums and musicians do about their music. Unfortunately, that emotional attachment often means we're blind to the errors we make when we're writing and can create a feeling that the book is far better, or worse, than it is.

How do we combat that?

Emotional distance. That means taking a step back, putting our work at arm's length, and giving ourselves some time and space to detach from the emotional high that comes from finishing a book. None of this is to say your book isn't good (I hope it is!), but you need clarity when you start the editing process or else you will be tempted to keep everything exactly as it is, thank you very much, and not want to change anything. Either that, or you will hate *everything* you wrote, hate your life, and want to delete it all and start over. Or go live in a cave somewhere and leave literacy to other people while you scare the locals as their newest cryptid. Hey, I've had that urge, too. Being a bog gremlin is a life aspiration of mine.

While I'm sure there may be people in the middle somewhere, I've rarely ever heard of an author who was "meh" about a book they just wrote. After all, if they are just "meh" about it, they rarely do anything with it after writing it, or never finish it to begin with.

How do we create emotional distance? Usually, it's a function of time. Once you're done writing your draft, it can be tempting to immediately jump into editing it. An experienced writer may do just that. I sometimes do. But more often than not, I give myself a few weeks or a month to enjoy the rush that comes with finishing a book before I start editing it.

Take some time to savor the feeling of accomplishment and do *just* that. You should feel good. Writing an entire book is a major accomplishment that a relatively small percentage of the world ever completes. Even with the millions of books published each year, the percentage of the population who finishes a manuscript is tiny. If we look at the number of people who do NaNoWriMo, even, only between ten and fifteen percent of people typically finish the challenge.

Of course, NaNoWriMo is its own, unique beastie, and it's not a perfect analogue to the number of people who write globally, but it does give a little perspective on the number of people who finish books after starting them. As an aside, with NaNoWriMo's issues recently, I don't really advise anyone engage with the organization until they've had a chance to sort themselves out, assuming they do.

Once you've finished basking in the feeling of having finished your book, it's time to dig in and get to work. If you can read your first few pages without either wanting to crawl into a hole and die or tell everyone you are the world's best author, you can probably start the process.

One final note on the emotional distance angle: This also means you shouldn't feel too horrible about your book, either. If discovering that you've made some awful typos or turned a scene into word salad harshes your calm to the point where you want to quit writing, you aren't in the emotional and mental space to start editing. Editing is a blow to the ego sometimes—even more when other people start editing your work—so understand that you'll need to be ready to laugh at yourself, have a square of chocolate, and reaffirm that you are a human and not ChatGPT. And even ChatGPT makes terrible mistakes on the regular.

Tools and Programs

Self-editing is *hard*. There's no way around that, and there's no avoiding it. It's a reality. Our brains tend to read what we meant to write more than they do what we actually wrote, and half the time, we want to bang our head on the desk and shout, "Why am I so bad at this?" because it feels like every mistake is a personal failure.

If that sounds like something you've experienced, the good news is that you're in the company of every author on the planet. I recently was working on a manuscript I've written and said someone tied their boat to the "mooing" rather than the "mooring." After some groaning, I sent a screenshot of it to my editing friends, and we all got a good laugh out of the resulting mental image.

Self-editing is not something you need to handle by staring at your manuscript until 3 a.m. questioning your sanity, or at least not *only* that. There are, in fact, many tools available to help you self-edit your book. *However*, none of those tools replace a flesh-and-blood editor because, while these tools are excellent, they cannot help you with creative issues. And sometimes, the advice they give is just plain wrong.

As intriguing as the world of artificial intelligence is, until my autocorrect stops trying to change things to "ducking," I am never going to be out of a job.

Before we get into the tools segment, one thing you will notice is that I don't include ChatGPT on this list. I strongly recommend avoiding AI editing for things more complex than punctuation, and even then, it gets *that* wrong sometimes. While some of the tools on this list include AI in their underpinnings, AI does not (at the time of writing) have the ability to really edit a work effectively.

Furthermore, if you put your novel into ChatGPT or other such AI generators, you're feeding the language model your entire book. That means someone else could pull from it when using generative AI to create something. If that prospect doesn't make your hair stand on end, then go forth and do whatever it is you want to do, but I don't believe in giving my data away for free where I can avoid doing so. Large language models might end up with my books in them due to skimming on the internet, but I'm not going to purposefully feed it to them.

Keep in mind that I am a Windows PC user, so there may be Apple-exclusive programs out there with which I am unfamiliar.

Microsoft Word's Spelling/Grammar Checks

If you use Microsoft Word, the innate spelling and grammar checks aren't half bad. Sometimes, their suggestions are questionable, so you'll need to actually think about whether or not it is making good recommendations, but it will catch things like whether or not a comma should be where it is a reasonable percentage of the time.

You can also give it rules you like and rules you don't. If you're a fantasy writer, or have a lot of foreign language or technical jargon, the dictionary can be iffy, but you can always right click a word and tell Word to add it to its dictionary in order to ensure it stops yelling about your main character Harmarang Frumplebottoms.

Grammarly

Grammarly is one of the top grammar checkers without a pulse, but it doesn't seem to be *that* much better, so if you have Microsoft Word and don't want to pay for Grammarly, you're not missing much. However, if you don't use Microsoft Word and, say, use Google Docs or Open Office to write in, then you might find it a useful tool. The premium version is better than the free one, but Word easily outstrips the free version. However, some people swear by it. Personally, I think it has more use for business purposes than it does for creative writing.

Hemingway

This program, in addition to basic grammar checks, will ping particularly long sentences and catch adverbs and passive voice. It's an excellent tool for a new writer to help identify these passages and errors in a visual way that you can use to improve your writing.

ProWriting Aid

I have no personal experience with this software, but from what I understand from others, it is a very useful one. It will mark things like overused words, cliches, and so on. It does more to pay attention to the flow of your writing than some of the others that are more grammar and punctuation based.

SmartEdit

This one I know very well. SmartEdit is my copilot for a lot of my editing work, and I swear by it. Like some of the others, it lists things like repeated words, cliches, repeated phrases, how many sentences start with specific words, and so much more. It comes in two versions, a Microsoft Word plug-in as well as standalone editing software. I personally attach it to Word because I have other such plug-ins that help automate some of the more tedious tasks I perform.

PerfectIt

Much like SmartEdit, PerfectIt is my other go-to piece of software. While SmartEdit catches things to do with composition and cliches and such, PerfectIt focuses on things like consistent use of words (toward vs. towards), and you can have it automatically check if quotation marks are curly or straight. You can also set up a style and punctuation guide that has things set how you like them, or you can have it conform to a style guide already in existence, like the Chicago Manual of Style, AP, MLA or APA etc.

Macros for Word

If you are using Word to self-edit in, you can get into the wild world of macros. While I am not a macro expert by any means, you can learn more about them from the website of the mighty and wonderful Paul Beverly, who creates many.

However, macros are more technical than the rest of these and may be a bit intimidating to learn at first. I am still dabbling, but most of the editors I know swear by them and use macros to perform a number of the tasks I rely on SmartEdit and PerfectIt for. Also, if you use Microsoft Word already, there are vast libraries of macros that are entirely free, whereas SmartEdit and PerfectIt come with price tags.

The Purdue OWL

While it's not a writing or editing program specifically, I would be doing you a disservice by not mentioning it. The Purdue OWL is an excellent resource to help you brush up on elements of punctuation and citation, depending on your needs. It is an extremely useful tool, and it is regularly updated to keep up with APA and MLA guidelines.

In addition to providing a wealth of literature, it also includes many exercises to help you put these things into practice and test your knowledge. It is an invaluable resource, and the fact that it is *entirely free* makes it one of the most valuable items on this list!

Types of Editing

Before telling you the specifics of how to do them, let's talk a little about the types of editing. Contrary to what most people believe when they start out, there are four different types of edits, each with a different focus.

The four types of editing are: developmental, line, copy, and proofreading. While many people conflate copy editing and proofreading, they are performed at different stages in the process and are separate steps with specific focuses.

Developmental Editing

This step in the editing process focuses on the big picture items. It looks at story structure, characterization, plot holes, worldbuilding, pacing, and other major pieces. If you're working in speculative fiction, it may include looking at the magic system in fantasy or the tech involved in a science fiction novel. It ignores things like word choice, punctuation, grammar, and so on to instead look at the work as a whole.

While it can be easy to say that this type of editing is subjective—and it is, to some degree—a skilled developmental editor can help you pave over plot holes, correct character issues, and strengthen your worldbuilding. You can also do some of this on your own (which we will cover in this chapter), but a good developmental editor is a must if you are finding yourself struggling with your plot or dealing with issues of a broader variety than just misplaced commas and adverbs. Also, a good developmental editor can be a game changer for those of you who are new to the process of writing. A lot of the time, it can be like taking a college-level course on craft and story structure.

Developmental editing is also called "substantive editing" by some editors and organizations. By some other organizations, line editing is *also* called "substantive editing." You might hear both definitions in your travels, so it's good to know the differences in opinion that can appear.

Line Editing

Zeroing in from the broad strokes of developmental editing, line editing is the art of polishing prose to a mirror shine. A good line editor is focused on bringing your voice to the forefront while eliminating unnecessary words, ensuring you are saying what you intend to say, and in general, just tightening up your book into a well-oiled machine.

This particular type of editing is my specialty, and I look at it as almost a form of gem cutting. Removing excess, noting places where the author needs to add more, clarifying things, and making the prose sing. A good line editor won't alter your voice as the author. Instead, they will enhance it and make the writing more *you* than it might be otherwise. Cutting away dead wood and polishing the heart of it until it shines is the work of line editing.

It's worthy to note that there is a gray area between line editing and copy editing, and different editors and editorial organizations sometimes call line editing "heavy copy editing." If you aren't sure how it's being defined by the person you're talking to, there's nothing wrong with asking.

Copy Editing

When most people think of editing, they think of copy editing. This is the process of cleaning up the syntax, grammar, punctuation, and clarity. It typically won't include removing excess words, fixing things like passive voice, or any of the rest. It focuses instead on the mechanical aspects of correcting the work.

While it is entirely possible to do this without doing line editing, many line editors tend to fold copy editing into what they do (as I do) as part of their process. However, doing things like ensuring the quotation marks are facing the right way is often a separate pass through the document rather than trying to do it while correcting the rest.

Proofreading

This is the absolute last set of eyes that goes onto a document before the public sees it. Proofreading is done by someone with a "proof" copy most of the time. In this digital age, it often means seeing the document in the form in which it is being sent to the printer or ebook formatter.

Proofreading has the lightest hand of all the types of editing and is exclusively focused on fixing things like formatting errors, last-second typos, quotation marks facing the right way, and other such things. They are the small errors. In most publishing companies, the proofreader is a different person than the editor who has been working on the document otherwise. This means that the final pass is done by someone with fresh eyes and not done by someone who has already read the book multiple times and may be blind to the small errors.

Proofreading also checks for things like ensuring indentation is done properly, fonts are correct, page layout is right, and there are no widows and orphans visible in the manuscript. Things like that.

With these four types of editing, you can, of course, have folks who do pieces and parts of each one, and you as the author will be performing three (up to proofreading) before you do anything with your book except work on it yourself. You want to do all these things before sending it to beta readers or sharing it with anyone but an alpha reader or two. Or your book coach, if you hire one.

Fortunately, this gives a bit of a guideline as to how many times you should go through the manuscript before setting it aside: probably a maximum of three. If you go through it a million times, you will lose perspective and not be able to see the forest through the trees. Even more so since you are the author.

Some authors go through their manuscript many more times, but if you find yourself doing back-to-back-to-back edits, you should set the book aside for a time—a week, a month, whatever. During that break, find other things to work on. Perhaps work on your marketing platform, start another project, whatever it takes. Then, after some time has gone by, come back again and take a look with fresh eyes. You can repeat that process as many times as you need, but trying to do it all in a marathon may cause you to lose that emotional distance we talked about in the previous section.

Self-Developmental Editing

When dealing with a manuscript that is over *sixty thousand* words long, it's easy to feel like you don't know where to begin and get sucked into minutia while ignoring the bigger issues. This is why I always advise authors do things in very specific passes to focus on their self-edits one step at a time. Trying to do all of it at once is a very quick trip to frustration and stress. Not to mention missing things.

Once you have more experience, you may be able to combine certain elements of the editing process and condense it to suit your personal flow. There is nothing wrong with that, and there are multiple approaches to doing so. However, when you are just starting out—as this book is designed for—you shouldn't try doing too many steps at once or skip steps because you will end up overwhelmed.

For what it's worth, professional editors also don't combine all the steps into a single pass, either. If we are doing multiple types of editing on a single document, we usually do multiple passes through it while focusing on the specifics of the type of editing we are doing.

Unlike with writing, where some folks like to bounce around scene to scene and write whatever they're excited about at the time, you should do editing in a straight shot, front to back. If you bounce around, you run the risk of missing things or introducing continuity errors into the story. While *writing* doesn't need to be linear—though I strongly suggest you consider doing so since it makes editing easier—editing absolutely has to be.

The first time you start edits on your manuscript after writing it, you are going to be doing a developmental pass on it. This means you keep your grubby little mitts to yourself and just read. The exception to this is if you see an obvious typo you can correct with ease. Don't start rewording things or reworking them. Ignore all that. Your goal with this pass is to look at the big picture items.

If you *do* see things you want to change like a continuity error, instead of actually changing it, make a comment in the margins, whether digital or handwritten, and note what and where. Save yourself the headache and don't start editing things on that level right now. Your whole job for this read-through is just to see what's on the page before changing it.

While you read, write a bullet-pointed outline of what happens in the book, chapter by chapter, and note major events. You can do this part on a piece of paper or in a separate document—whatever works best for your brain. This is extremely important. It might feel silly to write an outline of something you already wrote (and maybe wrote an outline for the first time), but there's a method to my madness. Trust the process.

You can and should *also* make notes of things you want to change or issues you notice. Does a character mysteriously stop being a smoker halfway through the story? Does a character's gender need to change? Did a character change species by mistake? Make those notes either along with the outline or in a separate notebook. I tend to write my outline in Word and take notes about things I want to fix either on paper or on my e-ink tablet, but whatever you feel works for you is the method you should use.

Once you've read the entire book, start to finish, and made notes and your outline, review the outline and notes. Do you see any obvious issues with the plot? Characters? Pacing?

You might have noticed scenes that drag or things that you want to rewrite all together because they don't conform to everything else. Or you may have identified places where a character walks out of a room, never to be seen again. We all have those moments, so don't be unkind to yourself about them. Just mark them and note that they need fixing.

Self-Editing

At this point, you might have a pretty hefty volume of notes to go through, and all the more power to you! After the first read through, start implementing the changes you identified as needing to be made. Remember, though, we are focused on the broad strokes stuff. If you want to shore up a specific description or wrangle commas, you can, but remember what I said about separate passes. If you start micromanaging at this stage, you might neglect more meaningful edits.

Finally, you will want to use this pass to fact check yourself about locations and data. If there's anything you aren't sure of, double-check things to ensure you are as correct as you can be within reason. If you're dealing with fantasy, this might include things like looking up how certain weapons are used or cared for. Or horses, for that matter. If it's sci-fi, you might want to check into the science a little. If you're writing crime fiction, it may require you to check on how CSU handles crime scenes or various statutes and legal elements that you need to make sure you get right.

This is the phase where some authors end up rewriting the whole manuscript. If you end up in this place, don't despair. I have several books on my computer that I have rewritten at least once and will rewrite at least one more time from top to bottom before they ever see the light of day. While it can be frustrating to realize you need to gut and reorganize the entire book, it doesn't mean you're a failure. Sometimes, you have to smash the clay back into a ball and make a new pot because the one you were working on had a wobble. I don't even want to talk about the number of times I've had to "frog" an entire crochet or knitting project and start it over again because I got stuck somewhere. It's just part of the reality of creative pursuits.

Self-Line Editing

Before you think this is going to be just another book telling you to delete adverbs and use nothing but "said," please know that none of my advice here is to be taken to an extreme. I'm also going to explain *why* certain things are said so you can understand the principles rather than just hearing the advice everyone parrots. The why of it all will get you a lot farther than just the what.

While I do believe certain words are of limited use to writers in certain circumstances, limited use isn't *no* use. My suggestions are to be taken with the understanding that I am not you, and my writing is not yours. If my recommendations don't make sense for your book, you can ignore me. However, the principles I lay out have pretty universal application so far as I have found.

Also, I know this isn't a craft book, exactly, but the next segment is going to dig a little deeper into craft in general as it comes to word choice because that's absolutely necessary for this segment.

"That"

The word "that" is frequently used as a filler. I'm not saying the word has no function whatsoever, but its function is specific. While you absolutely can insert it in many places in a paragraph, please understand not all of them need it to make sense. With that in mind, you should be conscious of its use so you don't lean on it too heavily.

There are circumstances where you cannot avoid it, but unless you need it for clarity, or to reinforce a character's voice in dialogue, I would consider specifically avoiding it for a while and seeing what you can create without it.

As an example, I'm going to rewrite the above paragraphs adding "that" everywhere it could be used to illustrate my point.

> The word "**that**" is frequently used as a filler. I'm not saying **that** the word has no function whatsoever but **that** its function is specific. While you can absolutely insert it in many places in a paragraph, please understand **that** not all of them need it to make sense. With **that** in mind, you should be conscious of its use so **that** you don't lean on **that** too heavily.

> The word "**that**" is frequently used as a filler. I'm not saying the word has no function whatsoever, but its function is specific. While you can absolutely insert it in many places in a paragraph, please understand not all of them need it to make sense. With **that** in mind, you should be conscious of its use so you don't lean on it too heavily.

The difference isn't extreme, and it can be somewhat taste-specific, but you can see the difference between the two paragraphs if you look. You don't need to delete "that" from your vocabulary, but using it consciously will make sure you don't end up overusing it by mistake.

Also, as you may notice, the second paragraph is four words shorter than the first, so it's a way to help drop word count without harming content and tone if you apply the principle throughout the book.

"-ly" Adverbs

No, I'm not going to pry them from your cold, dead hands. The places I suggest you avoid using them is *when they replace a stronger verb*. There are times and places where an adverb is just the correct word, but so often I see it used to either modify a weak verb, and thereby replace a stronger one, or cause a statement to be redundant.

For example, I would always advocate a stronger verb if you wrote, "He ran quickly." There are so many options out there that would make it stronger: sprinted, charged, rushed, tore, or even "hauled ass." Avoiding these weak verbs punches up the action and reduces your word count.

When dealing with redundancies, I would say "he whispered quietly" is redundant in the sense that whispering is inherently quiet. However, if someone whispers *loudly*, as in a stage whisper, that might be worth noting.

As with almost everything else on this list, the key is intentionality. Write with purpose, and choose your words with care. If the right word for the spot is an "-ly" adverb, use it. The key is to think it through and do so with an understanding of why the choice matters.

"To Be" Verbs

This includes am, is, are, was, were, be, being, been. These verbs are not inherently bad, but they can be symptoms of other problems such as "telling" or passivity. Much as with the "-ly" adverbs, we need to use these with intentionality.

Telling isn't all bad; sometimes, you need to get a point across quickly. However, if you lean on these and don't do enough showing—or the story is mired in passive voice or passivity in general—you will discover it damages the pacing, so make sure you think about these things while writing. It also can add wordiness.

This recommendation *does not* apply to dialogue since people talk using these verbs all the time. But in prose, we can usually avoid them by adjusting things a little. Below is an example showing the principle:

> Alberton **was** a small town that **was** perched on the edge of a cliff. The view **was** beautiful. The town overlooked a valley that **was** full of flowers, and it **was** a great place to live.

> The small town of Alberton perched on the edge of a cliff. It overlooked a valley full of flowers and **was** a great place to live.

Neither of those are literary genius, I know. But with some light reorganization, you can see it went from thirty-six words to twenty-six words and reads tighter, cleaner, and smoother without losing any of the information since saying "the view was beautiful" is redundant. That's an example of what I'm getting at with the to-be verb removal. Obviously, they can't all go for clarity's sake, but where it was easy to rephrase the sentence to remove it, the impact is heightened, and the wordiness is culled.

"Very," "really," and other unhelpful modifiers

Again, this is not about dialogue. But "very tall tree" versus "towering tree" mean almost identical things, and "towering" is a far stronger word. There are times when "very tall tree" might be the better phrase (children's literature comes to mind), but those circumstances are not the norm.

You might have caught onto a trend here where saying precise things in fewer words is better than saying wibbldy (yes, that's a word now) things in more of them. Being concise and specific is both good for your word count and for your reader. It also creates clearer mental images for them without wasting a lot of page space. To quote the Bard of Avon: "Brevity is the soul of wit."

Redundancies

These are things like "nodded her head" and "shrugged her shoulders." You can't shrug your head and nod your shoulders. If you can, I have deep concerns about your anatomy. Some actions are only performable with specific conditions. It would be like saying, "She thought with her brain." That doesn't work well, either.

Furthermore, saying things like, "It was cerulean blue," is also redundant. Cerulean is a kind of blue inherently. And you can't have cerulean red, after all. These sorts of things can be cut out wholesale without damaging your narrative.

Excessive dialogue tags

Dialogue tags are great. They help readers know where they are in text, but often, writers use more than necessary. Using action around the dialogue can help contextualize it and identify the speaker.

Also, I'm not one of those people who think "said" is the only dialogue tag. However, I don't think every line of dialogue needs a flowery description to it, either. I would save those things for when the dialogue really needs an extra punch of importance rather than using them constantly. You don't even need a dialogue tag at all if there's action in the paragraph or if it's clear who's speaking. Below is an example of an exchange with no dialogue tags whatsoever.

> "Stop the car!" Callie flailed her arms, trying to get the driver's attention.
>
> When it pulled over, the driver rolled down his window, scowling at her. "What in tarnation are you doin'? You're gonna get run over standin' in the middle of the road like that."
>
> "The road's out around the bend." Callie pointed toward the sharp curve down the road. "There's a sinkhole."
>
> "Damn."

As you can see in the demonstration above, dialogue tags aren't required for every single piece of dialogue. They might not even be necessary in an entire exchange if it's short and clear. Keep ones that improve clarity or add flavor to the text, but as a general rule? Ditch as many as you can without confusing people.

Overly specific descriptions of non-important things

Don't have your action take place in a white void. That said, if you are in a place where the description doesn't need to be detailed, don't do it. The same goes for people. Add things that provide characterization, but a laundry list is not going to help, and too much specificity chokes the imagination out of the reader. You can also provide broader descriptions such as describing someone's clothing as "goth" or what have you and allow the reader to fill in details. Or you could describe someone as wearing a band T-shirt, or having something specific they're wearing rather than every detail of their wardrobe.

Let's do an example of too much description and then one of that description pared down:

Self-Editing

> Moxie stood 5'6 and had red hair down to her butt that she kept in a series of thirty-two tight braids filled with green, white, blue, silver, brass, and metallic orange beads and black elastic bands at the ends to hold everything in place. She had a band T-shirt on for the band Megadeth with holes on the front, around the collar, at her elbows, and a few scattered across her belly, and she wore white Sketcher's sneakers. She wore green eyeshadow and red lipstick along with blush and mascara. Her jeans were black and also had holes in the knees and thighs. Her belt was black leather and buckled with a silver buckle on the third hole.

Conversely:

> Moxie was 5'6 and wore her waist-length red hair in tight braids studded with colored beads. She wore a well-loved Megadeth T-shirt, ratty jeans, and a pair of Sketchers. Her green eyeshadow accentuated her green eyes, and red lipstick drew my attention to her full mouth.

Now, some of this is a matter of taste. Certain genres call for more description than others, but note the details I kept and the details I left out. Her belt being leather is probably unremarkable unless leather is a rarity in your setting, or she's got the same belt as a killer or something. Exactly where the holes were on her shirt and jeans are unlikely to matter a great deal unless we're doing a crime scene analysis. Same with the specific number of braids and the exact color of the beads and elastics.

There *are* times where excessive detail can be important to a story. If you have a Sherlock-type character who is doing a deep analysis of a crime scene, there might absolutely be a reason to dig into every single detail of a character's description. However, outside of them doing active analysis, you don't need to provide that level of detail for every single character or set piece you come across.

In addition to these things, while you are doing your line editing pass, you're going to want to identify scenes and passages where you may have not written enough. Often, writers come in two flavors when it comes to first drafts. There are those who write *everything* down and then have to cut out a bunch, or you have folks who write spartan drafts and have to insert a bunch of extra things in order to not have the story taking place in a white void. I am the latter camp, so I have to study my book and know where to explain or describe things in addition to making sure I haven't overused any of the above conventions. I also rely on my beta readers to tell me where I need more description.

Remember, this pass is about making the way you use words shine, so concentrate on *how* you convey your story and what methods you use to ensure you give the reader the best experience.

Self-Copy Editing

Doing self-copy editing is the simplest piece of all of these elements, but it requires some of the most technical knowledge. If you are self-copy editing, there are a couple ways of handling it. You can use the self-editing software I mentioned in the earlier section, or you can get really cozy with the Chicago Manual of Style (CMOS) and try and learn it all yourself.

Keep in mind, also, that copy editing software regularly makes mistakes, so even if you run it through that software, you'll want to examine each and every change it suggests and consider whether or not it's correct.

I don't have any specific tips for doing your own copy editing beyond studying the CMOS, reading things like the Purdue OWL, and/or checking out Grammar Girl's website. Going through your manuscript for errant commas and quotation marks facing the wrong way is by far not the most exciting of the self-editing passes, but it is just as important as the rest.

How to Stop Editing

One of the most important things about doing your own editing passes is knowing when to stop. We writers often fall into the trap of wanting to tinker with our books forever. We make small changes and fuss over details and keep working on them for eternity to avoid the act of sharing them with anybody.

Sometimes, this tinkering is because an author doesn't know when to stop, but others? It is a reflection of the fear they feel. If they're editing it, after all, they don't need to show it to anybody or look down the barrel of (gulp) publishing it.

We can all relate to this fear because all of us have been there. There's no shame in the fact that you're afraid of sharing it with the world. We all fear the rejection of something we have poured dozens, if not hundreds, of hours into and that we feel is a large part of who we are. It often feels like someone rejecting our book or critiquing it is the same as them rejecting *us* and who we are as people.

The good news is that most of us feel that way. Creative work naturally comes with a lot of rejection. *Every* author receives bad reviews at some point. If you're pitching to publishers or agents, you *will* get rejected. Not every beta reader will enjoy or even finish your book. There are also writing groups where you can post passages and have them torn apart by other writers with varying degrees of helpfulness and compassion.

If you post your work online using a service like Wattpad or Royal Road—which I strongly advise against if you ever intend on publishing the work for money—readers might say unkind things. Or, almost worse, they might not say anything at all.

It's okay to not want to ever get past the stage of having written something for your own pleasure. You aren't obligated to show your book to anybody, ever, if you don't want to. You can write it and just be proud of having written it. There is absolutely nothing wrong with that. However, if you *do* intend on publishing a book, whether this one or another, you are going to have to overcome that fear of other people seeing it, put on some armor, and get ready to be vulnerable.

That also means stopping editing. As I said in the previous section, I strongly suggest not doing more than perhaps three passes through a manuscript at any given time because you will quickly become blind to errors and end up seeing only what you *intended* to say rather than what you said. Your book will not be perfect after three passes, but there's only so much you can do alone to perfect your book. And at a certain point, "perfect" becomes the enemy of "good."

A finished manuscript is a million times better than something you never stop tinkering with (or, worse, never write) because a finished manuscript is *completed*. You don't need to write the Great American Novel to have done something worthwhile. If you're still worried about your book after having done a couple passes, stop fiddling with it. Put it away for a while and come back to it after some time has passed. Then keep at it.

If you really feel like you've hit a brick wall, there are options out there, like hiring a book coach or contacting an editor to do an assessment on it. Some editors, like myself, offer manuscript assessments for a reduced rate and will read through a work and give general feedback and offer some insights into things you might need to work on. It won't be the depth of a full edit of any type, but it will give you some direction and insight. A book coach is someone who can talk you through what you're stuck with by providing you with a certain number of sessions or beta reading to help you identify things that you need to work on or break through barriers.

Those services are not extremely cheap usually, but if you are at your wits' end and can't break through the barrier into the next step (beta reading), it might be worth seeking some professional advice.

Summary

This chapter gets deep into the subject of self-editing and goes over ways you can work on polishing your early drafts. We went over different tools and programs that exist, the types of editing and how to do them on your own, as well as when to stop editing and turn the book in already. As I said at the outset of this chapter, this is not a replacement for professional eyes, but undertaking this process can save you a *great* deal of money when you reach the point of working with a professional!

Key Takeaways

- You cannot edit something if you are too emotionally close to it. You have to give it some time to sit before you start working on it because otherwise, you will either hate everything or love everything; there is very little in between.
- There is a large array of tools you can make use of for editing your works, and you can explore the ones you like best to add to your toolkit.
- Understanding that editing is broken down into multiple types, each with different focuses, can help you break down the task of editing your book and guide you as to what order you should undertake each task in.
- Self-editing techniques will only work if you have a strong understanding of craft.
- There comes a point in every writing journey where you have to stop editing and start the next stage of the process. Knowing when you have reached that point is vital to your ability to continue moving forward.

Chapter Six
Beta Reading

So what is beta reading, anyway, and what good does it do? The answer is: a lot.

Beta readers are the folks who are going to see your finished and polished draft before you send it to anyone else. These people should not be your immediate family and friends—unless they're authors or editors themselves—because you need people who aren't going to spare your feelings. While you don't want people who are going to be cruel to you, of course, you absolutely need folks who will be honest with you if there's something they don't like.

Before you start your adventures in beta reading, however, you will need to finish your manuscript and likely do a couple rounds of self-editing to try and polish it as much as you reasonably can before sending it on to fresh eyes. If you want feedback on the earliest stages of your book, what you're looking for at that point is *alpha* reading, not *beta* reading.

Why Beta Readers Matter

The reason you need beta readers is, of course, to make sure your work connects with your target audience and ensure the story makes sense and flows. Their function is absolutely vital to the process, and their contribution to the overall product is marked.

Your beta readers should be people in your target market. We haven't talked too much about that term prior to now because it's one I'm mostly going to be talking about in the second half of this series, *How to Publish the Damn Book*.

To summarize it in the loosest terms, your target market is the people you hope will read your book and enjoy it the most. Don't make the canon mistake of thinking "everyone" will enjoy your book (nor should you go up against a Sicilian when death is on the line). No book is enjoyed by literally everyone. In fact, most books are only enjoyed by a fraction of the overall population who like the genre and are interested in that kind of story.

For example, the book you're holding right now has a target market of newer writers who may have written one book or not finished one at all yet. This also presumes the reader is a person who has an appreciation for snarky humor, terrible puns, and my more casual method of writing. Strunk and White, this ain't.

Whatever book you're writing, you want beta readers who represent that target market to read it. If people who *aren't* your target market read it, they may not enjoy it for reasons that have nothing to do with the quality of your writing or narrative, which renders their feedback marginally helpful.

If I asked my uncle, who only reads non-fiction and spy thrillers, to read my Regency Era fantasy romance novel and give me feedback, he couldn't. Not that he wouldn't support me—I know he does—but he's not the kind of person who would usually enjoy that kind of book. And he probably wouldn't enjoy mine, even if he was sweet about it.

Working With Beta Readers

Working with beta readers is a little like a precursor to working with an editor, so learning how to interact appropriately with them will save you a lot of headaches later. There are a number of things to know about working with other people when it comes to your book, but the most important has to be this:

Leave your ego at the door.

I cannot count the number of times I've seen an author absolutely implode when they share their work for feedback and receive critique. I get it. It stings to hear someone doesn't think your book is the best ever. It really does, and it won't get better when you start receiving reviews that may not view your work favorably.

However, you absolutely must check your ego. No matter how much it stings when someone gives you that kind of feedback, you need to step back and examine it with an open mind. Not everything you'll hear will be useful, but remember: These people are reading your book and spending time to do so in good faith.

This isn't to say you need to use, keep, or employ every bit of advice you receive, and if someone is *not* acting in good faith, you don't need to be their punching bag. If I had someone come after me for having LGBTQIA+ content in my books and attempted to force me to remove it, I absolutely wouldn't. However, if someone is not providing feedback such as that, it's inappropriate to react in an adversarial way.

So, without further ado, here are my rules for the care and feeding of beta readers.

Be Appreciative

Seriously, appreciate them. Beta readers are taking time out of their life (about seven or eight hours, often) to read your book for the express purpose of trying to help you with your writing journey. That's the thing.

They are often doing this for free, and they are doing it entirely with the desire to help you. Being appreciative and respectful of their time is absolutely necessary! Make sure you thank them for their time and effort, even if the feedback you receive is not extremely useful.

Also, part of the reason to be good to your beta readers? They're *part of your market*. If you're a jerk to your beta readers, you'll get a reputation that will haunt you forever. Having a reputation for being a jerk is not something you want, *particularly* not at the start of your career. Being gracious and appreciative of people's help is a step toward ensuring your public relations remain positive.

Be Respectful

This might often be bundled with the top one, but being respectful should be the baseline for all your interactions with your beta readers and other members of the writing community. You don't have to agree with them, but don't be rude. If you have a meltdown and lash out if someone gives you well-intentioned but critical feedback, you are not going to do well when your book is exposed to the public. Recognize that this is, in fact, a litmus test of what it's going to be like when the public reads your book.

This respect also extends to things like how long it might take them to read the book. Sometimes, reading takes a while, and these folks are doing this in their free time, unpaid. They may not be professional grade, or they may be very busy. If that's the case, be patient and willing to accept that things may take some time.

Hiring a beta reader is actually a service out there that exists, and if you're working with a paid individual, they should provide you a timeline and be a professional. Even then, though, you want to remain respectful and considerate of their time and expertise.

Don't Argue

Just don't. Arguing with beta reader feedback is pointless because they are both giving you their *personal opinion* (which they're entitled to, whether you like it or not) and because you are not going to change that opinion. You cannot convince someone to like something they don't. No amount of my mother's efforts to convince me to put less sugar in my tea made me enjoy my tea that way, and there's nothing to be done about it. I still take my English Breakfast tea in a standard sized mug with three lightly rounded teaspoons of sugar, thank you *very* much.

Arguing with your beta readers just makes you come across as both immature and rude. Their feedback doesn't have to change your book, and you don't *have* to use it, so why fight with them? Thank them for their time and efforts and move on. Also, if they're not into the book they just read, they probably won't be into others you write if it's the same genre, so you can remove them from your beta reading pool.

If you *do* have all the feelings about their feedback, you're entirely allowed to drown your sorrows in a tub of ice cream and your favorite television show. Sulking is a time-honored tradition. Just make sure you don't take your beta reader down with you.

Don't Overexplain

If you find yourself having to explain things to beta readers before or while they read the book, it could be a function of your anxiety. Further, if you spend a lot of time explaining things to them, you aren't letting them read the book in a clean space, so to speak. You're tainting the pool by adding information that may not be in the actual book. If you have to do that for them to understand the story, then there's a problem.

Trust your reader to be smart enough to put the pieces together because, when your book goes out into the real world on its first big day of school, you aren't going to be there to explain to readers what you meant when you said things. Nor should you try.

If your beta readers ask you questions that you need to explain, take note of those questions and consider addressing them in the book. But those explanations should only be given when requested of you and maybe only given after they've finished reading the story.

Provide Content Warnings When Applicable

This one is *very* important. If your book deals with themes that might cause someone to experience significant emotional distress, make sure you tell people that before they read it. While I have deep feelings on the specific phrase "trigger warnings," providing people with a heads-up is not out of your way, nor does it spoil anything.

In general, if you don't know someone, and aren't aware of any particular trauma issues they may have, you should use content warnings for graphic depictions of violent acts, graphic discussion or depictions of things that can evoke specific trauma (such as miscarriage, self-harm, eating disorders, etc.), and graphic gore or sex. Think of it like you would watching an episode of *CSI*. They put a warning on the screen if an episode discusses specific themes that could be harmful to people.

It shouldn't have to be said, but working with beta readers is just working with people. Providing base respect, appreciation, and kindness shouldn't have to be pointed out, but I see folks becoming defensive and combative so frequently that it is worth reinforcing.

I get that emotions can run high during beta reading. Particularly early on when you aren't feeling secure about yourself and may still be learning. It's easy to posture and fluff up your feathers rather than accept being wrong.

Neuroscience shows that such things elicit actual fight or flight responses in us. It's all right to have those emotions. Everybody does. It takes time and repeated exposure to get used to having those experiences. There is nothing wrong or abnormal about that.

The key in all this is *to not take it out on the people who are trying to help you*. And that's who your beta readers are: people trying to help. If you discover yourself unable to cope with feedback without having feelings you cannot mitigate, drown in ice cream, or otherwise step back from, you might not be able to cope with the realities of publishing. At least not right now.

There's no shame in that. Just make sure you aren't making those feelings everyone else's problem.

Where to Find Beta Readers

This is a question a lot of folks ask, and it can be hard to answer at times. Beta readers should be, as previously stated, people who aren't your immediate circle of friends and family unless those friends and family happen to be authors or editors themselves. As a professional in the sphere, my friends are those people, so I'm lucky. However, when you're looking for beta readers and haven't yet built up the network, it's time to start.

Looking for beta readers can happen several ways. First, you could look for writing groups. Whether in person or virtual, writing groups offer a place for writers to gather, talk shop, and commune over the fact that we have *strong feelings* about the Oxford Comma. Not every writing group is designed for every person, and you might need to try multiple before you find a place to settle in.

Meetup.com has a number of listings of writing groups that meet in person. Your local library may also have a writing group who occupies some slice of it at various times. You can also try local college campuses to see if there are any writers' groups who gather there. If not in person, Facebook has many, many writing groups of all different types and flavors. Some focus on a specific genre or subgenre while others are broader. You can also try Discord, where there are many servers dedicated to writing (such as my own, the Insomniac's Workshop). Instagram has an active writing community, as does TikTok.

If nothing else works, you can *try* asking your friends and family, but you're going to need to understand that if they don't read it or don't like it, they may be afraid to say anything for fear of hurting your feelings or damaging the relationship. So make sure you ask people you can trust to give you honest and straightforward feedback.

Finding your people isn't something I can just send you a list for, unfortunately. It will take time and effort.

If you don't want to go the route of cultivating relationships with writers and developing friendships to have them beta read for you, there is the avenue of paying someone. There are, in fact, paid beta readers and services, like me or my friend, Crystal Watanabe of Pikko's House.

These services often run around $100 - $300 USD or so (depending on length) since you're asking a professional for about eight hours of their time. It's not free, after all. You may be able to find inexpensive ones on places like Fiverr, but *caveat emptor*—when it comes to services like this, you typically get what you pay for.

Alternatively, you can get a membership to a website like BetaReader.io, which is a site dedicated to helping writers and beta readers connect. I haven't used that one myself, but I've seen it mentioned frequently enough online that I feel comfortable including it.

What to Do With the Feedback

When your beta readers (and you want multiple) come back with what they think of the novel, take all the information they give you, read it, and save it. Then wait a little while. If this sounds a little bit like the "emotional distance" advice I gave about editing, you'd be exactly correct. The first time someone says they don't like your book or find elements of it confusing or boring or what have you, it is going to sting like road rash. That is just how it is. It *will* hurt.

Give yourself a little time to regain your emotional distance before you start thinking too hard about their feedback. You can use that time to pout, write out of spite, weed a garden, scream obscenities at the universe... Hey, I'm not going to tell you what to do with your day.

One way or another, when you feel more settled, start re-reviewing the feedback. Evaluate it for a few things: whether or not it's just a matter of opinion, if multiple readers are saying the same thing, if you agree with the feedback and realize there's an issue, or if the feedback is unhelpful. The feedback that fits that last category can be disregarded. Things like saying that you should delete all the commas from the manuscript for *artistic merit* would fall into that "unhelpful" category.

Unless you've hired an editor to beta read for you, beta readers are not usually experts in the craft of writing. While they should be trusted to tell you what they do and don't like, they often fall flat when they tell you exactly how to fix it because *they're not experts*. If they *are* experts, be doubly grateful for their feedback but also know that some editing calls are a matter of opinion. If you hire ten different professional editors, you will receive as many different flavors of editing when it comes to certain elements of your book, particularly when dealing with story and style elements.

To that point, sometimes, things beta readers pick up on will be a matter of taste. Certain readers may or may not like specific tropes, conventions, or characters. They might prefer stories that go a different direction. There is nothing wrong with that, but those opinion-based pieces of feedback are best taken with a grain of salt. Some of those things may be important (like including a happily-ever-after or happily-for-now in a romance novel), but other elements may not be as germane, such as an individual who does or doesn't like morally gray protagonists. Those sorts of opinions are entirely fair, but you don't need to conform to everyone's preferences to write a book your audience will love.

The things you're really looking for are the places where the beta readers agree. If multiple people gave you similar feedback, you really need to examine that thing. For example, if multiple people said your main character was difficult to relate to, that's something you're going to want to resolve. They may disagree on how they'd fix it (and a lot of the time, they'll give you their opinion whether you asked for it or not), but if several of them hit on a specific point that they found difficult, it warrants your attention.

Also pay special attention to the places readers say are boring. If they peg a part of the book that just doesn't keep their attention, you should examine it closer for pacing issues or make sure that you aren't dropping large swaths of exposition.

This feedback is gold to you because, while beta readers aren't typically editors, they're providing you with extremely useful services and giving you a snapshot of what the public will think of your work. That insight and knowledge is invaluable. Even if it does sting some to receive.

If you discover that the feedback is that folks universally don't enjoy the story, please don't take that as an indication that you should quit writing altogether and instead take up underwater basket weaving. Critical feedback presents you with an opportunity to learn and grow. If the feedback is well-intentioned and has a good point, you ought to treat that like liquid gold. The beta reading phase is the perfect opportunity to continue honing your craft and moving onward.

If you have to go back to the drawing board on a few things, that's also *entirely normal*. Don't despair if your beta readers send you back into rewrites because that's a common experience. You can bounce between rewrites, self-editing, and beta reading a few times before you ever release a book.

Summary

Beta readers are an invaluable part of the writing process and are vital for you to get early feedback on your manuscript before it's shown to others. Their work should be treated with respect and appreciation. It's okay if it stings and makes you want to throw things at times. Just remember that their intention is to help you!

Key Takeaways

- Beta readers are your first opportunity to see what people who aren't in your immediate circle think of your book.
- Your beta readers should be people who would otherwise read similar books to yours; if they're not, they may not be able to provide the feedback you need.
- Working with beta readers is similar to working with other professionals and requires that you treat them with respect, appreciation, and practice the way you will handle editorial feedback from others.
- Not all beta feedback is useful to you! It's okay to not apply things that don't fit your book or your message.
- Finding beta readers can mean looking online or in your local community for places where writers gather. You can also hire professional beta readers if need be!
- Take some time to sit with the feedback after you receive it. Much like with self-editing, you need to create some emotional distance before you start digging in to address the things your beta readers noticed.

Chapter Seven
Final Touches

After you've gone through your rounds of beta reading and editing based on the beta readers' comments—assuming you need to—it's time to consider your next steps. At this point in your journey, you should have a book that's as close to finished as you can make it on your own. This is decision making time.

The next book in this pairing, *How to Publish the Damn Book*, discusses the paths to publication and the routes you can take, but I'm going to give you a little bit of a preview here because once you reach this phase, you're going to want to start thinking about things to come in the future.

With the rise of indie publishing and self-publishing since the late 2000s and early 2010s, the industry has seen a massive boom of books being published. This is a double-edged sword because while indie publishing has allowed voices traditional publishing has often not welcomed to be heard, it has also resulted in the "slush pile" being made public. In publishing, the slush pile refers to the query inbox at a publisher or literary agency. It is a hive of scum and villainy.

All of this to say, since Amazon threw open the gates, everything has a home there. *Everything*. While I don't in any way have anything against indie publishing—I'm doing it myself with this very book—we do need to be mindful of the environment into which we are entering.

I also want to state in clear language that, regardless of the route you take, there is no wrong answer. If you decide you don't want to release your book for money and just want to upload it on a website somewhere (Wattpad, Tumblr, Royal Road, AO3 etc.), there is nothing wrong with that. However, if you *do* intend on publishing it, there are three major paths we'll review in this chapter.

With that, let's talk next steps.

Considering a Series

If you've written one book, you should give some thought to whether or not you intend to make something a series. The answer could be, "No," but keep in mind that authors often have to release multiple books before they get much attention—which translates into the number of sales one is likely to make. It takes time to build up an audience, and sometimes, that means multiple books. If you're writing non-fiction, this may not hold *as* true, but this book is mostly focused on fiction authors, so that's why I'm sharing this piece of advice.

Whether you write a series or a number of stand-alone works, think about what your next steps are in terms of writing. A series is *one* of the things that can help sell because you will have something called "read through." It's what it sounds like: the fact that people will start at book one and continue through to the other books in your series. Simple enough.

I'm not going to focus *too* much on the business stuff here (that's the next book in the series... see what I did there?), but if you *are* considering a series, you will want to create something called a series bible. This is a document where you store all the worldbuilding information you have created.

I use Plottr for this purpose and have character profiles, factions, and the rest all in there so I can pull from it in order to ensure continuity in the series. That continuity is important because if I change a character's age, eye color, etc. between books, it will make readers twitch. And we don't want that!

The more complex the book, setting, and metaplot, the more important a series bible becomes. Regardless of what genre you're writing in, you will want to keep those notes, but a series bible is absolutely necessary in the speculative fiction genres where we are often writing about places that aren't modern-day Earth. Or, if we are writing about modern-day Earth, we might be doing something with it that requires extra information, knowledge, and insight.

There are multiple methods for keeping a series bible, and none are wrong, but you will want to set up a system that includes, at minimum, the following information:

- Character profiles with physical attributes
- Faction information
- Important locations and their descriptions
- Racial/species attributes for fantastical creatures
- Rules of your world (such as magic or sci-fi limitations)
- Timeline of events for important moments

One of the things I also use Plottr for when creating a series bible is keeping a detailed outline of previous books so I can refer to it when writing. If I need to know what happened in one of my previous novels, I don't need to re-read the whole thing or try and remember the details; I can look it up in Plottr on the timeline and put it together.

While I will never stop singing the praises of Plottr for this purpose, I know folks who have used OneNote, a series of .txt files in organized folders, a personal wiki, World Anvil, and many other methods to keep track of all of these moving parts. Some folks use Word files with headings to link to various subsections. These methods are all usable, but you'll have to play with them to find out which works best for your brain.

Writing a number of stand-alone novels in the same genre (this is common in romance, for example) is also a perfectly valid strategy. What I don't advise is writing a ton of books in entirely disparate genres with nothing to connect them because getting your readers to move from one of your books to another will prove a significant hurdle. If you write one fluffy romance novel and one hard-hitting military sci-fi and then a YA portal fantasy, the amount of crossover in those audiences is very, very small, so you will have to market each individual book to an entirely different market and reinvent the wheel every time.

As I said before, not every author needs to write an entire series. You might prefer stand-alone novels or even a singular non-fiction book. Just give it some thought because, as I will explain in the next book in *this* series, the business of it makes good sense for writers.

Paths to Publishing

Most people buying this book, I suspect, intend to publish their work one way or another. While there likely are alternatives to what I'm going to say, I've been in the publishing business a long time now, and in my experience thus far, there are three viable paths to publishing. None is inherently superior to the others. They are all equal but require different things and have different benefits and challenges.

I'm going to do my best to enumerate the various different options here and give you a frank view of what the paths mean for you as the author so you can make the best choice for yourself.

The three paths are:

- Big Five Traditional Publishing
- Indie Traditional Publishing
- Self Publishing

I should note that there's *technically* a fourth in which you do some combination of all of the above pieces like a 'mix-and-match buffet. That doesn't require much explanation on its own, however, so just understand that if you *are* going to go that route, all this information may be of varying degrees of use to you.

Let's just dive in without wasting more time on preamble.

Big Five Traditional Publishing

As I write this, the Big Five (Penguin/Random House, Hachette Book Group, Harper Collins, Simon and Schuster, and Macmillan) are looking at a merger to become the Big Four, but that's uncertain and is currently facing anti-trust issues in the courts. I'm not sure where that situation will be when this book goes live. Also, by the time you read this, they might even be the Big One. I can't prognosticate.

This path to publishing is the one most people think of when they think of becoming an author. You get an agent, pitch your book to the heavy hitters in the publishing industry, get an advance (if they choose you), and have your book distributed everywhere. They may even invest money into your marketing and advertising—*may*—if they think you're a good bet to make. While this route is the one likely to get you on bestseller lists and won't cost you money up front, it is a route that comes with significant hurdles as well.

Pros:

- You will be seen by everyone as a "real" author.
- The Big Five are likely to throw at least a marginal marketing budget at you in some form or other.
- You will likely receive an advance if you are selected.
- Your book will be distributed everywhere.
- Your book may be translated into multiple languages and/or have an audiobook made.
- You are more likely to get onto a bestseller list.
- Having a publisher means you will be taken more seriously by certain marketing outlets.
- Your book will be produced and published by a team of consummate experts in the industry.

Cons:

- You are likely to make very small royalty percentages (10-15% off net).

- Your agent will take a cut of your advance and royalties, depending on your contract.
- You lose creative control of your work as well as subsidiary rights, such as film adaptations.

- The querying process can be agonizing.
- If your book isn't what they want right now, you won't be published.
- You must meet certain sales benchmarks to be considered for future books.
- You will still be doing a lot of your own marketing.
- You have very little say over any decisions made about your book, including editing.
- Marginalized people often have trouble finding representation and may be left by the wayside.

I'm not trying to rag on major publishers here. Don't get me wrong, there are plusses and minuses, and if Harper Collins slid into my DMs offering me a deal, there's a good chance I'd take it. But one must be realistic about the drawbacks, too. Major publishers are in the book business for one reason only: to make money. The good news is that they know what will make money. The bad news is that you may not always like or agree with what they believe.

Indie Traditional Publishing

The rise of indie publishers has been something I've watched since I got into the business. I started working in the industry for an indie publisher, and I then graduated to running Insomnia Publishing before I switched gears to focus on offering services to authors directly. This is where my experience lies. I'm sharing this to be transparent about any biases I may have that favor this particular option, but there are genuine drawbacks, too.

Pros:

- Potentially will not require an agent to receive publication.
- Your book distribution will be managed by the publisher.
- Your book may be translated into multiple languages and/or have an audiobook made.
- Having a publisher means you will be taken

- more seriously by certain marketing outlets.
- Your book will be produced and published by a team of consummate experts in the industry (theoretically).
- You will often have more creative voice than you might with a Big Five publisher.
- Negotiation for copyright and subsidiary rights is more likely.
- Potentially better royalty rates than the Big Five.

Cons:
- You are likely to make small royalty percentages (15-30% off net).
- You may lose creative control of your work as well as subsidiary rights, such as film adaptations.
- The querying process can be agonizing.
- If your book isn't what they want right now or isn't timely, you won't be published.
- You must meet certain sales benchmarks to be considered for future books.
- You will still be doing a lot of your own marketing.
- You have very little say over any decisions made about your book, including editing.
- There are sharks in the water; not all indie publishers are trustworthy, and hybrids require a LOT of extra scrutiny.

As you can see, there are benefits and drawbacks, and many of them resemble those of the Big Five because they are still publishers. Indies often take more risks than the Big Five do, and finding an indie publisher who focuses on a specific group of marginalized voices is vastly more likely in indie publishing than it is in the Big Five. The larger indie publishing companies also have marketing budgets and will give you a similar marketing push to the Big Five, if at a smaller scale.

I want to note again that there are sharks in the water. If an indie publisher sounds too good to be true, they are. Make sure you read your contracts and, if you can, have a lawyer look at them to make sure everything is above board. No legitimate business will tell you not to do that and, in fact, most of us will encourage it.

Hybrid publishing, where authors pay part of the cost of publication, can also be a place for vanity publishers to hide since many of them have rebranded themselves as "hybrid." There are legitimate hybrid publishers out there, but you need to be *very careful* to vet them before you agree to anything. Otherwise, you'll end up with the newest iteration of Publish America.

Self-Publishing

This method has gained popularity steadily over the recent years, and it can create a phenomenal opportunity for authors to avoid the gatekeepers and publish their work themselves.

While you absolutely *can* do this on the cheap, it's not something I recommend because that often results in a sub-par product unless you are ingrained into the author community and have contacts who will work for you inexpensively but do the job well.

As such, I am writing the pros and cons below with the understanding that this is going to be something you pay for, not just self-editing and putting it up on Amazon.

Pros:

- Author receives 100% of the profits.
- Full creative control of your book (for better or worse).
- No need to query or find an agent.
- If you have a series, you are the only thing determining if it is finished or not.
- Control over your release dates and times and methods.
- Decision making about your book's distribution channels is in your hands.
- No gatekeepers.

Cons:
- Full creative control of your book (for better or worse).
- Expensive (often upwards of $2,000+ per book).
- Need to find your own team and vet them.
- All marketing and advertising is done on the author's dime.
- No publication support you do not pay for.
- Need to arrange for distribution on your own.
- Must understand and make all business decisions.
- Often not taken seriously as a "real author."

Self-publishing is a viable way of getting your book out there. Despite the stigma that still refuses to have the good grace to die in a corner, it's just as valid as traditional publishing. The downside comes in the form of having to pay for all the things that traditional publishers cover. Because that's the core difference between traditional publishing in all its forms and self-publishing: who foots the bill.

The reason authors make what they do from a traditional publisher is simple: the overhead costs of putting a book out are not cheap. Most traditional publishers invest around $10,000 of equity into a book. From editing to typesetting to cover design to the ISBN and distribution, all those various steps cost money. And it is not cheap.

I mention this because you can go the cheap route, but it's the difference between someone recording themselves playing music on a cell phone microphone and going into a recording studio. Can you do it the first way? Yes, you can. Some people even make money out of it and end up big. But does it produce the best possible product? Absolutely not.

Perhaps it's because I'm a professional editor of many years, but I feel very strongly that, if an author cannot afford to put equity into their book-—because it's a *business*—then they should not self-publish at that point in time.

It's okay if you can't afford to hire an editor, cover designer, typesetter, and so on. But if you can't, you should give serious consideration to traditional publishing because putting out a poor-quality product is often worse than putting out nothing at all.

There you have it! The three major paths to publication. I'm going to provide a far more in-depth discussion of the options in the next book as well as how to take each of the steps you need to in order to go from manuscript to print, but a preview of that decision here will give you an idea of the various possibilities until you (hopefully) buy the second book.

When to Start Marketing

Marketing is a reality for all authors because, if you want people to buy your book, people need to know about it. I'm not going to go deep into marketing here, but I do want to give it a nod because it's a question that comes up a lot, and it's a reality you should be familiar with before you get too deep into publishing territory.

Regardless of which of the various paths you choose, you are going to need to become intimately acquainted with marketing if you intend to publish your book for money. So when do you start?

The answer is simple: You start now.

Building your author marketing platform is a far larger creature than just yelling "buy my book!" from every pulpit you come across and in every venue you find. It's far more than slapping your cover into reading groups and walking away. Building your marketing platform is going to be something that takes time, and there's no time too early to start.

So what do you do? What are the steps you should take?

For now, there are just a few small things I strongly suggest you do in order to begin your journey into marketing:

- Buy your author name as a URL, even if you

don't have a site yet.
- Create your public-facing social media profiles, even if you don't know what to post.
- Consider what your brand will include. What of yourself do you want to share with the world?.
- Network with people in the writing industry (writing groups, professional organizations).
- Start reading about marketing for authors.

If you start doing those things now, you will find it far less overwhelming when you get close to publication. They may seem large and scary, but you honestly don't need to *do* much just yet. At this stage, you want to start considering the meta questions and making friends. Because nobody is better at hyping your new releases than other authors.

Networking and making friends with other authors and with professionals is going to get you a lot of mileage, and it will result in you having a far stronger understanding and network when you're ready to release your book. That networking might be joining a few authors groups and asking questions or sharing experiences with people. It might look like joining a Discord writing community. It could take a lot of forms, and you aren't obligated to choose any specific one. From BookTube to BookTok to Facebook groups to LinkedIn, there are so many ways to meet authors who write similar things to you that you have many options to choose from.

Also, if you start reading and studying the concepts now, you will find that it is far less terrifying when you get rolling because you will know what's needed in advance. It's far less scary driving to a new place if you have a map, after all. Don't wait until your book is out to learn the business aspects of publication. You have all the time in the world to make these decisions and study this industry, and starting early will make you far more likely to succeed and remove a great deal of the anxiety of the unknown.

Networking also helps with that because you'll meet people further along in their journey who can give you some insights and help you along the way. In general, the author community is a "rising tides lift all ships" sort of place (yes, that *is* a reference to 20BooksTo50k™). We aren't in competition with each other, after all, because in the time it takes us to write and publish a book, a reader will have devoured a dozen or more. I can read an average-sized novel in a few hours if I'm really in a groove.

There's no way one author can satisfy the appetite of a reader, so there's no competition. We're all in this space together, and if we lift each other up and encourage one another and share the road? We all win.

Final Considerations

This book contains a lot of information. I wrote it to be as direct, to the point, and focused as possible because that's how I think. Being autistic, I need clear instructions when I embark on a journey. There are a million and one books out there on craft, but I discovered there were very few that ever gave me a direct, straightforward path to writing a manuscript.

I obviously cannot cover every single aspect of the complexity that is writing a book in this one space, but it is my sincere hope that I have provided you enough to take some of the mystery, fear, and stress out of the process.

At the very end of this book, you will find an appendix with useful resources, people, and works that I have collected over the years—including my own website, which has links to my Substack, author newsletter, and more.

If you still have questions or are struggling, you can reach out to me directly—my email is on my website. If I get an overwhelming number of emails, I may be slow to reply to them (and I'm so sorry about that), but it's my genuine desire to help as many people as possible find success. If writing a book is something your heart has wanted to do and you have been working toward that end, I hope you will find this resource useful.

From the bottom of my heart, I welcome you to the author community, and I hope you will find support, success, and a career that will push you toward your personal goals. Success can be ephemeral and hard to pin down, and it looks different for everyone, but whatever your goals are, I want to encourage you to chase those dreams. Just do so in a way that is realistic and grounded in knowledge.

Appendix

My personal website contains information on writing, editing, marketing, and more. To locate it, visit me at: http://www.ehprybylski.com.

Joining my twice-monthly newsletter will also get you a regular infusion of writing and marketing advice to your email inbox, plus a free short story!

Books on Craft

- *On Writing* by Stephen King
- *Sin and Syntax* by Constance Hale
- *The Deluxe Transitive Vampire* by Karen Elizabeth Gordon
- *Save the Cat* by Blake Snyder
- *Save the Cat Writes a Novel* by Jessica Brody
- *The Anatomy of Story* by John Truby
- *The Anatomy of Genre* by John Truby
- *The Snowflake Method* by Randy Ingermanson
- *Writing the Other* by Nisi Shawl and Cynthia Ward

Writing Software

- **yWriter**: http://www.spacejock.com/yWriter.html
- **QuollWriter**: https://quollwriter.com/

- **Scrivener**: https://www.literatureandlatte.com/scrivener
- **Plottr**: https://plottr.com/

Editing Software

- **Grammarly**: https://www.grammarly.com/
- **Hemingway**: https://hemingwayapp.com/
- **AutoCrit**: https://www.autocrit.com/
- **SmartEdit**: https://smart-edit.com/
- **PerfectIt**: https://intelligentediting.com/
- **Word Macros**: http://www.archivepub.co.uk/

Marketing

- **Jenn Hanson-dePaula**: https://www.JennDepaula.com
- **Quinn Ward**: http://www.WriteYourOwnPath.com
- **Tammi Labrecque**: https://www.NewsletterNinja.net
- **The Writing Wives**: https://www.TheWritingWives.com/

Want to learn more about publishing?

Join the AUTHORiTEA newsletter to claim your free sample of the next book in this series: *How to Publish the Damn Book*. It gives step-by-step guidelines on how to navigate the waters of publishing and bring your book from manuscript to store shelves.

Scan me!

Or visit http://subscribepage.io/AUTHORiTEA

Acknowledgments

My journey into book publishing has been shaped by so many people. Far too many to name individually. I am grateful to the editors, authors, and people in my life who support my writing. You know who you are, and to name you would take up pages and pages because there are so dang many of you.

In addition to the people who have been with me through my publishing journey, I want to thank my family for their moral support, care, and encouragement. Particularly my mother, Linda, who has always encouraged my creative endeavors and who got me started on my love for books by reading me *The Hobbit* as one of my first chapter books. I can still remember her reading the opening lines of it as she tucked me into bed at night.

To my husband, Jason, who has been my loudest cheerleader and who has sacrificed much to share this writing journey with me. He has always been the first person to share my triumphs and my pains. I could not imagine a better partner.

I also want to thank my editor, Mel Ngai, who has helped me make my prose better and saved me from many embarrassing typos over the years. Cassiel Approves +10

Finally, I want to speak to all the writers reading this. You are why I wrote this book. You are why I do what I do as an editor. My heart and soul belong to the writing world, and I am ever honored that people choose me to walk with them on their journey. Working with authors is holding pieces of other people's souls in my hands, and I cherish that sacred space I am allowed into in ways too great for words.